# How to Love a Black Man

# How to Love a Black Man

## DR. RONN ELMORE

**WARNER BOOKS**

A Time Warner Company

Warner Books, Inc., 1271 Avenue of the Americas, New York, NY 10020

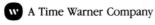 A Time Warner Company

Printed in the United States of America
First Printing: February 1996
10  9  8  7  6  5  4  3  2

Library of Congress Cataloging-in-Publication Data

Elmore, Ronn.
    How to love a black man / Ronn Elmore.
        p.   cm.
    ISBN 0-446-51878-6 (hardcover)
    1. Man-woman relationships—United States.   2. Afro-American men—
Psychology.   3. Afro-American women—Psychology.   4. Intimacy
(Psychology)   I. Title.
HQ801.E42   1996
158'.2—dc20
                                                                            95-34624
                                                                            CIP

*Book design by H. Roberts*

*To Aladrian, my wife, my treasure*

# Acknowledgments

My dream was to have a literary agent who would be as enthusiastic about this book as I. I pictured her to be a writer who could challenge my work, a reader who could understand my ideas, and a business partner with savvy to spare. Marlene Connor is proof-positive that dreams really can come true. I appreciate you deeply.

To my editor, Colleen Kapklein, who consistently offered me a unique blend of gentle sensitivity, razor-sharp insights and dead-on-target suggestions. I am a better communicator and this is a better book because of you.

Diana Baroni, Fred Chase, and especially Tammy Nichols added polish to the manuscript, making it truly shine. I am very grateful.

Special thanks to LaVerne Powlis Tolbert, my friend, former colleague, and writing mentor. When I was content to only stand and speak my thoughts, you demanded I sit down, shut up and write them—and you stood by to encourage me when I did. Were it not for you this book would not have been written.

Many thanks to my friend and brother, Charles Brooks, who often eased the pain of my frequent bouts with writer's block by his prayers, outrageous humor, and his generosity in providing me a quiet place to write.

I owe a tremendous debt of gratitude to Raedorah Dodd who patiently typed and retyped my drafts, then guided me from the era of scribbled notes on yellow legal pads into the computer age. You did it all with your characteristic creativity, and amazing grace under pressure. You are all I could ever hope for in an administrative assistant.

Sincere thanks to Isidra Person-Lynn of KACE Radio in Los Angeles, who dubbed me the "Relationship Doctor," put me on the air, giving me instant access to thousands who wanted help to strengthen their relationships, but might never make it to my counseling office.

To my pastor, Dr. Kenneth C. Ulmer, and the Family of Faith, whose unceasing love and encouragement continue to nourish and sustain me.

My parents, the Rev. A. J. and Ann Elmore, my brothers, Alvin, Gordon, and Larry, as well as my in-laws, the Rev. Joseph and Elizabeth Slade, have generously poured their love into my life. Neither my tongue nor pen could adequately express my appreciation to all of you for your special support and encouragement as I wrote this book.

There is no way I could have written knowledgeably and practically on love relationships with Black men, if it were not for my therapy clients and what working with them has taught me. Their lives, struggles, courage and their hope are the reasons for this book.

My children, Corinn, Christina, and Cory, are the delights of my life. You tolerated the rigors of my schedule and the special demands (and absences) that were a regular part of the writing process, and you did it with a kind of sweetness and caring that often overwhelmed me.

"Thank you," or any of its most lavish synonyms, could not do justice in expressing my gratitude to my wife, Aladrian. For every night you went to bed alone, suffering the sounds of my pecking at the computer, for saying, "Yes you can" with your eyes, when my heart said, "No I can't." For keeping my secrets and sharing my life; I am touched, I am honored, I am immensely thankful. Your way of loving this Black man is just what this book is all about.

Finally, to my Lord and Savior Jesus Christ, who gave me the idea, the ability, and the words to write this book. That You are honored by this offering is my heart's desire.

# Table of Contents

# How to Love a Black Man

# Introduction

Have you have found relationships with Black men to be mostly romantic, intimate, and mutually satisfying? Or complicated, mysterious, and frustrating? Whichever may be the case, this book has been written for you. Act on the practical advice offered here, and you will experience much more of the former, and much less of the latter. Period.

An extravagant promise? Certainly. But true nonetheless if you are anything like the countless women I have met through my counseling practice, seminars, and on radio and television talk shows where I have discussed Black men and the women who love them. No doubt your experience with them has confirmed that Black men are neither exalted deities to be worshipped, nor hopeless bundles of defects to be discarded. You are aware that neither view is in keeping with reality. Neither helps—him or you.

You already love Black men, and you plan to continue. Yet too often you have found that loving them has left you baffled, scratching your head, pondering lots of unanswered questions. You love Black men, but you can't swear that you always understand them.

You have rightly assumed that if you understood him better, you could love him better, and both of you could find deeper satisfaction.

When I say "love," I'm talking about a well-balanced and deliberate heart commitment to another person, one that is demonstrated by action. Action that benefits your partner without discounting yourself. Action that is sensitive, creative, and meaningful, without being self-devaluing, manipulative, or excessively self-protective.

And when I say "satisfaction," I mean the abiding contentment and confidence that result from committing to love someone, feeling loved in return, and knowing and doing the actions that effectively demonstrate your love.

Deeper satisfaction—for you and for him—is what this book is all about. It's an honest look at what works and what doesn't to achieve that satisfaction, and the things you can start (or stop) doing today to ensure you get more of it, more of the time.

So, you may well ask, "Are women, in some way, more responsible than men for the care and feeding of a mutually satisfying relationship?" Absolutely not. It takes both of you. It always has and always will. *How to Love a Black Man* explains what it takes on your part. It's only half the story. But it's the half that's yours.

Rest assured, this is not *1001 Ways to Stroke, Coddle, and Pamper a Man*. Do away with those ridiculous images of him reclining regally in a canopied chaise lounge while you hand-feed him grapes, fan him with ostrich plumes, and massage his feet—all at once.

*How to Love a Black Man* is an advice book. It's not as much a "think about it" as a "do something about it" book, and its advice is only truly effective when it is lived, not just learned. It's your guide to the very powerful things that you can actually *do*, not just consider, hope, or feel, but *do* to help you experience the kind of love you both desire and deserve. It may be the missing piece of the puzzle that you've been trying so hard to solve.

Yes, this book is about Black men, and for the women who love them. But it is *not* an examination of what's wrong with us in love. It is a celebration of what's right with us, and how to make it better than ever.

Here at the outset may be the best time to address a nagging and inaccurate suspicion that sometimes haunts this subject matter. Allow me to put it plainly:

This book should not be thought to imply that Black men, or the women who love them, are plagued with certain psychological, behavioral, or relational dysfunctions that are only found in our race and culture.

I have not written with that erroneous belief in mind, and I caution you not to read it with that in mind either. Getting and keeping a meaningful and mutually satisfying love relationship is no easier or harder for Black folk than anybody else.

*How to Love a Black Man* is written by a Black man, for women who love Black men. Self-help books by therapists focusing on the "mysteries of the male" fill bookstore shelves and the best-seller lists. Those books, however, usually proceed from a decidedly Anglo context. Both the images, and the vernacular, are resonant of Anglo culture, written in Anglo terms and for an Anglo audience. It's not that they are of no benefit to African-American readers, but it's like wearing borrowed shoes— you can get them on all right, but they're never *really* comfortable.

The concepts, images, and terms you will find here are rooted in the rich relational style and strengths that are characteristic of Black men and women. Simply put, it's about love, the way we see it, say it, and do it.

Many women admit to having grown at least a little tired of the whole subject of loving Black men. Still open-minded, but tired. Motivated, but tired; hopeful, but tired. Sometimes even sick and tired, but definitely tired. Are you tired?

- Tired of getting lots of the blame, and none of the credit for why he is the way he is? Or . . .
- Tired of the blizzard of disheartening statistics and analyses about Black men that are the topic of both talk shows and beauty shop debates? Or . . .
- Tired of waiting for the right man, at the right time, with the right kind of love to offer in return for your own? Or . . .
- Tired of your emotions feeling like an amusement park with only one ride—the roller coaster? Or . . .
- Tired of thinking you know him "inside and out," only to discover he has a third mysterious dimension that you really don't know at all?

My hope is that you, like the women I have been privileged to work with one-on-one, will find refreshment and renewed excitement about your relationship with the Black man in your life (or the one on his way).

I promise no magical solutions here, but you should expect these "absolute essentials" to work, and to work well. They will if you will. So push up your sleeves, and take a deep breath . . .

Love and satisfaction are within your reach.

# PART I

# Reality Check

# Get a Grip on Who Black Men Really Are—And Aren't

Whatever the images that you have in your head of who Black men are will play like a constant, silent video as you read this book. Those images of him can either greatly help you or hurt you as you work with this book. For the next few pages, I challenge you to fine-tune your video image of him. Ask yourself, "Does my image exist in fantasy, nightmare, or reality?"

But reexamination of men and your perceptions of them is only a start. Following that will be your opportunity to look inward at your own approach to love. How well has it served you? Often our sincere attempts to give and get genuine love sadly miss the mark.

Beyond hope, high standards, and way beyond reality dwells a mythological figure, the Ideal Black Man. He has never walked the earth, yet he has garnered the love and devotion of many a woman. He is absolute perfection personified. No woman has actually seen him, though some women thought they had, only to discover that they had been sadly mistaken. Still other women have waited, sometimes with patience, often with frustration, yet clinging to the fantasy that this flawless specimen does exist and could soon appear.

## THE IDEAL BLACK MAN

- Incredibly fine . . . but totally unaware of it.
- Built like Adonis . . . but never stuck at the gym.
- Sensitive and gentle . . . but not *too* gentle; not a wimp.
- Completely honest . . . but won't tell me anything that hurts.
- Totally unselfish . . . but remarkably independent; doesn't need anybody.
- Financially secure . . . but doesn't have to invest time in staying that way.
- Intelligent and well-educated . . . but never acts "proper."
- Sexually dynamic . . . but only "in the mood" when I am.
- Highly spiritual . . . but keeps his God "in his place."
- Articulate, even eloquent . . . but sounds Black, never white.
- Able to solve every problem . . . but not a know-it-all.
- Completely dependable, never disappoints . . . but not (yawn) predictable.

THIS IS NOT WHO BLACK MEN REALLY ARE.

Far out on the opposite extreme from the perilous exalted image of Black men is the Raw Deal Black Man. He is the hopelessly negative view of Black men that some women hold. It's an image that is the result of unfamiliarity, disappointment, and cynicism. It can trip you up terribly because it breeds fear and resentment, but never love and intimacy.

## THE RAW DEAL BLACK MAN

- Utterly irresponsible.
- Manipulative/exploitative; violent/abusive.
- Lazy/undermotivated/low-achieving.
- Completely undependable.
- Noncommunicative/inarticulate.
- Uncommitted.
- Self-centered.

- Immature.
- Sex-crazed.
- Criminal.
- Unfaithful. Insensitive to women (especially Black women).

Be honest. Is there a little courtroom in your mind, where Black men have been brought up on these very serious charges? Perhaps just a few of the men in your life? Most of them? All of them? How many depends on the amount of hurt, disappointment, and fatigue you've endured—and how much, misinformation about Black men you've internalized.

Your pain can make stereotyping, pigeonholing, and generalizing about Black men awfully tempting ("he" becomes "they," "some" becomes "all"). Actually few men deserve to be placed in this category. It is as extreme and unrealistic as the previous one.

THIS IS NOT WHO BLACK MEN REALLY ARE.

Left with only the two previous images of Black men, you'll find satisfaction in love to keep eluding you. Those representations of Black men only exist in the imagination of the very naive and the very disillusioned.

## THE REAL DEAL BLACK MAN

- Gets much of his sense of self-worth from his performance. Skill, achievement, conquest, acquisition, and competency are key for him in virtually all areas of life—including relationships.
- Possesses a wide and varied range of emotions, many of which are not available for outward display. Often afraid, angry, lonely, proud, or weary.
- Has survived repeated blows to his manhood—personally and historically.
- Is often more competent in showing his love than verbalizing it.
- Treasures his space, freedom, and independence (which can appear to be selfish).

- Is violently resistant to real or perceived failure.
- Is familiar with and expects severe losses.

The Real Deal Black Man is made of flesh and bone—the remarkable and the regrettable. He alone has the potential of desiring and experiencing your love and lavishing his upon you.

THIS IS WHO BLACK MEN REALLY ARE.

# Take a Look at Your Approach to Love

*Love is best felt when one's eyes are closed.*
*But love is best given when one's eyes are wide open.*

—African proverb

Before we look at the "how tos"—the Satisfaction Actions—of loving a Black man, you may need to take a good look at yourself. If you do, you will discover that you can unknowingly sabotage the very satisfaction you desire in your relationship. You can set yourself up for disappointment. It's easy to do, but hard to admit.

The big problem with love is that to do it right you risk lots of rejection, consume lots of time, and expend lots of energy. Love makes you vulnerable. You really could get hurt (and nobody likes to hurt). On top of that, love does not offer any up-front guarantees that you will be loved in return.

## Love Substitutes

To minimize the risks, and avoid the pain, many women have opted for a safer alternative to real love—*love substitutes*. Love substitutes are the well-ingrained, automatic thought patterns and behaviors that you have learned over the years. Though not truly love, owing to your unique personality and experiences, you may be using them to deal with the complexities of relationships. They are usually born out of a distorted view of yourself, or men, or both, and are used to serve your own security needs.

Love substitutes do work to decrease the risk levels in your relationships with men. But love substitutes *never* work to build lasting intimacy and achieve mutual satisfaction. They *are* powerfully appealing. I will show you why when I introduce you to the five most common love substitutes. One or more of them may be exactly what you have used repeatedly in your relationships with Black men.

How exactly do love substitutes work? Consider this.

Your perception of Black men has been seasoned by your previous experiences with them and the meaning you have assigned to their behavior—positive and negative. How you see yourself and them will always affect how you relate to them.

I have found that many women have distorted perceptions of men, either from their own emotional baggage, unrealistic expectations, or from erroneous or incomplete information about men. If your perception of Black men is off target, your way of relating to them will be too. Which makes you susceptible to picking up one or more ineffective and ultimately self-sabotaging love substitutes.

If you see Black men as rare, must-have treasures, and yourself as a lucky but somewhat undeserving recipient of their affections, instead of loving them you may have become obsessed with pleasing them—your love substitute.

If you're a *Pleaser*, you've put Black men up on a pedestal, and you do all within your power to make them impressed with you. You are shattered when they don't live up to your unrealistic ideal or when you fail to earn their favor. Instead of satisfaction, you feel disappointment.

If you see Black men as a little too undisciplined, dull-witted, and ill-equipped, and you see yourself as clever, conscientious, and generally superior, instead of loving them, you may be prone to controlling them—your love substitute.

If you're a *Controller*, keeping a tight rein on your man and the relationship has protected you from chaos and exploitation. It has kept you feeling safe, powerful, and wise. Control works—until you find that men aren't willing to stick around for it very long. Instead of satisfaction, you feel abandoned.

If you see Black men as weak and needy, but well-meaning little boys, and yourself as strong, nurturing, and responsible, instead of loving them, you may be prone to rescuing them—your love substitute.

If you're a *Rescuer*, you've constantly offered your best "bail-him-out," "fix-him-up," and "turn-him-around" efforts to too many men who are always willing to let you rescue them, but not to repair them. Instead of satisfaction, you feel exhaustion.

If you see Black men as far too complicated, fascinating, or intimidating for you, romance will be out of the question. Instead of loving them, you may be prone to avoiding them—your love substitute.

If you're an *Avoider*, you've studied, analyzed, and discussed men to death, but you've seldom risked pursuing one to love. By hiding behind platonic friendships, you become every man's sister, and nobody's lover. Instead of satisfaction, you feel loneliness.

If you see Black men as trifling, egotistical, or adversarial, instead of loving them, you may be prone to bashing them—your love substitute.

If you're a *Basher*, failed relationships with insensitive and unloving Black men have left you hurting too much and too long to contain your negative feelings—and the condemning words that go with them. You're on a mission to make sure that they'll know better than to mess with you next time. Instead of satisfaction, you feel anger.

Women who have adopted love substitutes may be very sincere in the "love" they offer. They call it love, but the love that comes from Pleasers, Controllers, Rescuers, Avoiders, and Bashers is only a counterfeit version of the real thing. Love substitutes never bring lasting satisfaction in a relationship. Maybe safety, longevity, or peace, but never satisfaction. They can't. Love substitutes arise out of concern for yourself, not the other person. Your partner then responds by "loving" you in some equally self-serving way.

This may explain why you have been disappointed in loving a Black man in the past. He's looked out for himself and his safety needs, and you have looked out for yours. Of course it's tempting for him to blame you, and for you to blame him, but that hasn't made anything better.

The fact to remember is, you are much more likely to get the kind of sensitive, supportive, stable love you need if you give more of the kind of approving, affirming, admiring love your partner needs. Real love has a strange reciprocal mathematics: Give him more of his kind, and get back more of your kind. (Note: It doesn't even matter which of you starts first, the result is the same.) Then satisfaction is possible for both of you.

It is important to note that the substitutes listed here, and in the following pages, are generalizations—and exaggerated ones at that. They won't tell your personal story word for word, but much of what you find under one or more of these five headings will probably describe you. Don't be discouraged. Recognizing the patterns that haven't been working in your relationships is the first step toward establishing patterns that do.

In the next section we will take a closer look at these five most common love substitutes (there is an endless list of others). If you are bold and honest, you will be able to identify the one or ones that apply to you. Of course, none of the love substitute categories say all there is to say about one person's relationship patterns; and virtually no one uses only one of these substitutes. But watch for what rings true to you, about you.

Although it may be tempting to skip these pages and go directly to the Satisfaction Actions, resist. Face your own love substitutes head-on, through the descriptive profiles, the brief analysis, and the self-tests in the next chapter. Combining that with a reexamination of your perceptions of Black men will make the Satisfaction Actions much more meaningful.

In Part II, all seventy-three Satisfaction Actions will have one or more symbols, above the title, representing each Love Substitute. By the time you get there you will know well which Love Substitute(s) is yours. Watch closely. Wherever your symbol(s) appears, it is indicating a Satisfaction Action that you should consider high priority.

Open your eyes and plow ahead. It will be worth it.

# The Five Most Common Love Substitutes

## Pleasers

*Your love life's theme song: "You're Nobody 'Til Somebody Loves You"*

Marilyn met Emmet, a physician, when she was visiting a sick friend at the hospital. Emmet and Marilyn hit it off immediately. She was flattered that she had caught the attention of someone as desirable as Emmet. Marilyn was thrilled when he asked her out. She was, however, apprehensive about what this obviously intelligent, upscale, attractive man might think of her after an entire evening together, not just a few minutes of chitchat in a hospital corridor. The Friday they were to go out, Marilyn took off from work and spent the whole day preparing for her date. She made herself sick to her stomach agonizing over what to wear and the best way to style her hair. By evening she had a throbbing headache and was a nervous wreck, trying to rehearse what to talk about to hold Emmet's attention at dinner. Marilyn was consumed with trying not to blow this chance to have a man like Emmett. By the time he arrived at her door, Marilyn definitely did need a doctor.

According to her girlfriends, LaJoy is "a whole 'nother person" when she is involved with a man. She's centered, fun to be around, and acts like she could conquer the world. When she has a man in her life, nothing at all fazes her. When the relationship ends, she makes a complete about-face. Depressed and withdrawn, LaJoy takes to her bed, and doesn't even want to see close friends or participate in her normal activities. Though she never says it, she feels like a total failure. To LaJoy, having a man in her life makes all the difference in the world.

Pleasers spend loads of their time pursuing a Black man's love. They work diligently to be as sure as they can that they won't be overlooked. They try to do everything right, which of course means doing it the way they think he'll like it. They think that the surest way to get a man's love is to first get his approval. So they study men, carefully memorizing their tastes, desires, and expectations—and feverishly work to live up to them. They are hardly even aware they do it anymore. They shun men's criticism and instinctively know how to avoid their displeasure, by acting, dressing, speaking, thinking, and even feeling the way they suppose their man would want them to. They'll even go so far as to borrow his opinions and abandon their own so as not to risk his disapproval. They are very pleased when he is pleased with them. They believe he is a rare, must-have treasure without whom their life is incomplete, or at least vaguely unsatisfying. They put men on a pedestal, and in doing so put themselves down and believe they must strive to measure up. Their secret fear is that if he knew how they really are, he'd drop them in a New York minute! They worship men. Too much of their happiness is dependent upon them.

Pleasers:

- Are in love with love, and the trappings that go with it.
- Feel great about themselves when men show interest, and horrible when they don't.
- Are secretly very competitive with other women, and struggle with feelings of inadequacy around men.
- Have men and relationships almost always at the center of their thoughts, their conversation, and their emotions.
- Hope that having a Pedestal Man of their own will somehow make up for feeling like they are not Pedestal Women.

## Are You a Pleaser?

### *True or false?*

1. You tend to play a role around men, taking care to dress, speak, and act in ways that you hope will convince them you are okay—but these ways are very different from your natural "backstage" self. F

2. You do humiliating things to make or keep contact with men. Things that you are embarrassed about before you do them, but you feel you must do anyway. (You have been known to pursue a commitment from him in ways that could border on begging, for example.) F

3. You go out of your way to keep the relationship progressing along so that he basically only has to show up. T

4. You give up your money, your body, or your time in ways that you don't want to, but you do it because he wants it. T

5. You are constantly doing mental work to make plans for him to be more and more impressed with you. F

6. You settle for far less from him than you give out. You feel a comfortable balance when he "owes" you. F

7. You know exactly what you want from him, but you almost never clearly state it. T

8. You have become good at justifying, defending, and explaining away his mistreatment of you. The phrase "He didn't *mean* to hurt me" has become your motto. F

9. You are comfortable giving love and showing affection, but you have a hard time accepting his compliments and other affection. F

10. You let other important areas of your life (your career, health, friendships) suffer when you are in a relationship. F

11. Your mood is tied up with his behavior and his mood. You feel fine only when he is feeling and acting fine. T

12. You avoid showing negative emotions around him (anger, insecurity, jealousy, embarrassment) for fear he might not approve. T

If you answered true to *any* of these, you have some Pleaser tendencies that can, and no doubt already do, hinder your relationships and your life in general. The more times you answered true, the more deeply ingrained and acceptable to you this safety-seeking love substitute has become, and the more it shows up in your style of relating to Black men.

All of the seventy-three Satisfaction Actions to come are for you, but especially those that have the ▲ Pleaser symbol above the title. Pay closest attention to them, because for you they are the most needed—and the most likely to be denied, resisted, or dismissed.

### YOUR FANTASY RELATIONSHIP

He is the world's greatest, most wonderful, super-terrific-in-every-way Black man—and every woman knows it. He has chosen you, and you only—and every woman knows it. Every moment of every day for the rest of your life, you look, speak, and conduct yourself "just right," thus managing to maintain his devotion and affections forever. Now you proudly stand alongside him on his pedestal, and live happily ever after.

### YOUR PROBLEM

Low self-esteem. You really believe something is at least a little wrong with you if there isn't a Pedestal Man with you. Whenever he comes along, you are sure you will be just fine.

### AS YOU READ THIS BOOK

You will be tempted to see this advice as more stuff you need to do to win him over to your side. You will be tempted to pay close attention to the advice that you think might help you impress Black men, and you may resist the advice that calls you to challenge him, assert yourself, and be honest. You'll be inclined to pass up anything that you think might make men uncomfortable with you.

The benefits of the upcoming love lessons you need most will slip right through your fingers if you don't determine right now that you are already worth men's love and affection. You don't have to earn it, coax it out of him, or beg for it. You are worth it, simply because you *are*, not because of what you do. As you work through the seventy-three action ideas in Part II of this book, it will be helpful for you to remind yourself that nobody really is on a pedestal above anybody else.

Here are some vital steps to take as you move through this book:

ACKNOWLEDGE your Pleaser tendencies. Your love substitute may well be the trickiest of them all when it comes to applying the Satisfaction Actions ahead. Because if you aren't honest with yourself about your people-pleasing ways you'll just use my advice to earn more of men's approval. And if you keep that mind-set, your love life will still be lopsided—all give and little get.

RESIST the urge to pay attention only to the love lessons that challenge you to be humble, responsive, and supportive, ignoring the ones that call you to be assertive, confrontive, and willing to walk away if necessary.

EXPECT men who have only seen the Pleaser in you to be somewhat thrown off by the self-confident woman emerging as you apply the advice ahead. Push through anyway. Remember, you are not there to earn his love, but to offer yours and accept his.

COMMIT to another woman who will be an accountability partner with you as you apply the upcoming principles. So much of being a Pleaser has to do with denial and self-deception about your motives. Your partner is a sister-friend who has your permission to get in your face and yank you back into reality as needed.

## Controllers

*Your love life's theme song: "My Way"*

Cecilia abhors anything that smacks of bossiness, rigidity, or manipulative power plays. She sees herself as an assertive yet bighearted woman and secretly prides herself on her high standards, superior know-how, and meticulous attention to detail. Cecilia thinks her boyfriend, Clayton, has lots of potential, and believes that with her wise input, he has every chance of succeeding. Cecilia does, from time to time, get annoyed with what she sees as passivity and a lack of initiative in Clayton. She finds his style a little too "half-assed" and believes that if he really listened to her, she could "tighten up his program" considerably. Clayton loves Cecilia, but is thinking about breaking off their relationship. He often finds her to be a bossy, nitpicky know-it-all who's determined to reorder his life in her image.

Everyone looks to Saundra for advice. Her family, friends, and co-workers alike look up to her with respect for her uncanny problem-solving abilities and her generosity in giving guidance to others. Saundra considers herself a wise and compassionate friend and advisor. She gets lots of fulfillment from it. Saundra's husband, Terence, swears that if you don't follow Saundra's advice to the letter, she will "drop you like a bad habit."

Paula believes there is a right way to do anything, and to do less than that, or differently from that, is just plain unacceptable. Her closets, her desk, and even her weekend schedule are always in meticulous order. She gets defensive, and very angry, if she's ever caught making even the slightest mistake. Women who know her well call her "Perfect Paula" behind her back. Men who know her well don't call her at all.

All three of these women are Controllers. They use their many personal strengths to keep order and avoid chaos in their lives or from their men. They can't abide unpredictability, so they try their darndest to make everyone and everything work exactly the same way today that they did yesterday. If you are a Controller, you feel safest when you have the power to control all the details in your relationship with a Black man. Having control of love—and your lover—is so important to you that you are instinctively drawn to Black men who are at least a little lacking in self-initiative or discipline, but who are utterly captivated by yours.

Controllers have high standards and very precise tastes. Contrary to the stereotypical image you may have of them, Controllers do not, at first glance, come across to their men as loud, tyrannical drill sergeants. They usually adopt a kinder, gentler, though no less determined, manner. No matter how soft, sweet, and virtuous-sounding, when it comes to men, Controllers want what they want, how and when they want it, but they vigorously assure you that what they want is always in your best interest too.

Controllers:

- Are super-responsible, pragmatic, and hardworking. Their patience wears thin with men who aren't.
- Expect their men's love to be demonstrated by bowing to their standards, values, and expectations.
- Constantly try to convince themselves and others that they aren't manipulative, compulsive, or demanding.
- Tend to *talk* about their emotions rather than express them.
- Use silence, withdrawal, or departure to punish their man when he fails to do it their way.

## Are You a Controller?

### *True or false?*

1. Your most frequent complaints to the man in your life have to do with what he "should have known." F
2. You do not handle last-minute changes or spontaneous and impulsive decisions easily. F
3. You often get angry with him because he won't take suggestions from you, but takes the same suggestions from others. I
4. You hate having to remind him of something you've already told him, but you can't seem to not remind him. T
5. You get angry if he only gives you most of what you wanted, instead of all. T
6. You envy how relaxed and nonchalant he can be when you are in a panic. F
7. You feel most comfortable when there are clear rules, agreements, and standards maintained in the relationship. F
8. You constantly give reminders, double-check, or otherwise monitor how well he did something he told you he'd do. F
9. You pride yourself on how orderly and disciplined your life is. F

10. You get deeply disturbed if he abruptly changes or ceases doing something he has always done. F

11. You are very sensitive about being thought of as a bossy, pushy, controlling female. F

12. You are much more comfortable in relationships where you are looked up to and acknowledged as advisor, problem-solver, and resource person. F

If you answered true to *any* of these, you have some Controller tendencies that can, and no doubt already do, hinder your relationships and your life in general. The more times you answered true, the more deeply ingrained and acceptable to you this safety-seeking love substitute has become, and the more it shows up in your style of relating to Black men.

All of the seventy-three Satisfaction Actions to come are for you, but especially those that have the ◆ Controller graphic symbol above the title. Pay closest attention to them, because for you they are the most needed—and the most likely to be denied, resisted, or dismissed.

### YOUR FANTASY RELATIONSHIP

You are married to a Black man who is a male version of you. He has your perfect standards, your superior tastes, your penchant for details, and your flawless instincts.

### YOUR PROBLEM

Fear of the unknown and uncontrollable. You harbor a secret belief that you will suffer some unspeakable devastation or catastrophic loss if your man (and virtually everything else in your world) doesn't fit your vision for a well-ordered, emotionally safe environment. You drive men crazy with the rules you enforce, and the punishment you mete out for every violation of them. You drive yourself crazy too, because you work so hard to get him to think, feel, and act the way you want him to, and he resents you for it and goes on his way. Relationships with Black men eventually become quite a bore for you, because you are a stranger to spontaneity and joyous surprise—two of love's greatest pleasures.

### As You Read This Book

You will thumb through this book looking only for "proof" that will support what you have believed all along about Black men—that you need to control them to be able to relate to them. You will tell yourself that the parts of this book that challenge your own way of operating don't really apply to you, but to other women whose situations and strengths are inferior to yours.

Being such a devout perfectionist could make following the advice to come quite challenging for you. It would be just like you to require everything said to perfectly match your point of view or be discarded. You will, of course, seek to perfectly execute the advice that you do accept, and you will expect perfect results that will ensure a perfectly satisfying relationship. And if my ideas don't work according to what you see as perfect, and if you don't see how by your own efforts you will be able to make it so, you'll find little use for this book.

If you put the principles into practice, you will soon come to the realization that you don't have enough control to make sure that all those perfect things happen. Your standards are so impossibly high that you could be robbed of this great opportunity to learn to shoot for "good enough" instead of perfection all the time. For a Controller, the best thing you can do with the Satisfaction Actions is to aim for a new and refreshing level of mediocrity. Now is your time to pursue the plain, simple, ordinary, regular, and mundane. You need to relax more and settle for "pretty good"—from your man and from yourself. It's not passively resigning yourself to poor-quality efforts and poor-quality relationships. Far from it. You see, your "pretty good" is still what the rest of us call incredibly wonderful. Most importantly, "pretty good" is what's realistic and available. For a perfection-seeking Controller like you, this is the path to real life and real love.

ACKNOWLEDGE that you demonstrate some Controller tendencies with Black men. Your perfect self-image will struggle with the distasteful notion that you, alas, are like everybody else, in that you possess some less than admirable traits and behaviors—like the rest of us. But once you acknowledge them, you can begin to change them and move on to giving and getting some "pretty good" love.

RESIST the temptation to elevate yourself above the advice found ahead. Act, if you must, as if it applies to women like you, with a love life like yours. It does, you know. Your subtle self-perception of superiority, and your unique specialness that must be maintained at all costs, could keep you from achieving the humility you need to agree to try these Satisfaction Actions, and to benefit from them. As you read, keep reminding yourself aloud, "This advice is good enough, and I can give it a good enough try." You will then be in a position to discover for yourself that good enough really is good enough.

EXPECT yourself to constantly be looking for a clear cause-and-effect relationship between the advice given and the outcomes you desire. You could become obsessed with "if I do that, then this is what I must see happen." Love is not that neat, tidy, and rigidly predictable.

If you follow my upcoming advice, you should expect to see some fruit from your labors. But don't reduce love to a list of trigger behaviors, with you controlling the trigger. The messy part of relationships is that there are a host of other variables that count for much, like attitude, consistency, tolerance, and unique circumstances.

COMMIT YOURSELF TO:
- willingly taking a journey into the uncontrollable world of relationships with men, which includes new, sloppy, awkward behaviors as suggested ahead. Slow progress, second starts, and even failures should all be seen as perfectly acceptable.
- letting the man in your life be responsible for some of the satisfaction in your relationship. Let his slightly lower (than yours) standards be sufficient. (Note: Some of the Satisfaction Actions urge you to let go of your tight hold on that for which he needs to bear the responsibility and the consequences.)

## Rescuers

*Your love life's theme song: "The Clean-Up Woman"*

Angela swears she does all she does for Wayne, because of her deep love for him. He means well, she argues, it's just that he needs someone like her around to love him enough to get him together when he won't do it on his own. Currently (and chronically) Wayne is unemployed. On Sundays Angela goes through the classifieds, circling job possibilities for Wayne. She has already updated his résumé. On Mondays she calls and arranges interviews for him. On the day of his appointment she phones to make sure he gets up on time, then heads over to his place to choose his outfit, starch his shirt, and drive him to the interview. Angela constantly, and joyfully, reminds Wayne that if it weren't for her, he'd be up a creek without a paddle.

Sara's husband, Norman, tends to shut down and sulk silently when he is stressed about something. For days at a time he barely speaks to her and mopes around the house as if all is lost. It is at those times that Sara gets busy, hovering over Norman and questioning him repeatedly about what he wants her to do to make the problem go away. Since he refuses to give her much information, or make direct requests for her services, Sara starts doing "detective work" to find out what's gone wrong in Norman's life. She feels her love obligates her to deal with his problems for him, if he won't. Sara never sleeps well until she's figured out how to change whatever it was that made Norman stop smiling.

Rescuers are on a mission to "help" their men improve their lives and to keep them as safe as possible from pain and discomfort. They volunteer to be the means whereby their men get to experience all of life's good stuff and none of life's bad, as the result of their caretaking efforts for him. Love means keeping him from ever having to say "Ouch."

If you're a Rescuer, the great appeal of this love substitute is that the busier and better you are at rescuing and fixing him, the easier it is to avoid the guilt you feel when you fear you aren't doing enough for him. You also get to savor that intoxicating feeling of accomplishment you get when it looks like you are succeeding at remodeling him. Rescuers use caretaking to get their own need to be needed met.

Rescuing and fixing your man will make you feel indispensable and secure in your belief that as long as he needs you, he'll always love you too. But take a closer look and you'll spot the serious side effects of this safety-seeking love substitute. Rescuing and fixing always leave the Rescuer feeling:

- Alone. He will soak up the goodies, but never change his ways, and never manage to give back as much as you give out. Or he will soak up the goodies, get fixed, and walk away from the woman he "needs" and toward one he wants.
- Resented. Your fixing will eventually make him feel needy and dependent, so he'll reject, ignore, or show no appreciation for your efforts.
- Exhausted. He will become addicted to your rescuing and fixing, and progress to demanding more and more of it—ultimately more than you can possibly give.

## Are You a Rescuer?

### True or false?

1. On at least two occasions you have put yourself in financial jeopardy because you pulled your man out of a jam. T
2. Sometimes your friends have criticized you for letting yourself be taken advantage of by a man. F
3. You have usually been drawn to men who lack something that you possess in abundance (such as intelligence, discipline, money, know-how, ambition). F
4. You have experienced stress-related physical complaints when your partner's life is in chaos. F
5. You often struggle with guilt feelings over something you did or didn't do for your man. T
6. You do certain favors for him that you'd be embarrassed if anyone else knew about. F
7. You have had a pattern of deciding to break off a caretaking relationship, then going back to the same partner, to give him "one last chance." F
8. You have told lies to protect him from something. F

9. The Black men you have been in relationships with usually have some glaring problem that needs solving (chronic unemployment, substance abuse, legal problems, emotional immaturity, passivity). ⌐

10. You often make excuses to yourself and to others for your man's irresponsible or inappropriate behavior. ⌐

11. There has seldom been a twenty-four-hour period in your relationship with a Black man that you did not offer him some advice for his problems. ⌐

12. You spend almost as much time doing things for him as with him. ?

13. You experience anxiety or harbor resentment when he abruptly ceases to call upon you to perform a task for him that you previously did. ⌐

If you answered true to *any* of these, you have Rescuer tendencies that can, and no doubt already do, hinder your relationships and your life in general. The more times you answered true, the more deeply ingrained and acceptable to you this safety-seeking love substitute has become, and the more it shows up in your style of relating to Black men.

All of the seventy-three Satisfaction Actions to come are for you, but especially those that have the ● Rescuer/Fixer graphic symbol over the title. Pay closest attention to them, because for you they are the most needed—and the most likely to be denied, resisted, or dismissed.

### YOUR FANTASY RELATIONSHIP

You want a man who wants to be *your* caretaker. You would be thrilled for him to be just strong enough to give you some of the same kind of loyal, dependable, and very hardworking love you give. But you want your man to be just weak enough to not be able to make it without you.

### YOUR PROBLEM

Fear of abandonment. You are absolutely terrified of the man who loves you becoming the man who leaves you. You have come to the conclusion that the glue that will keep him with you is your making yourself indispensable to him.

### As You Read This Book

Because you are so tired and so annoyed by how one-sided the love seems to flow in your relationship, you are ripe and ready to hear about more balanced and mutually satisfying ways to relate to the Black man in your life. You'd love to be rid of your tiresome and humiliating love substitute, if only you could be guaranteed that he'll still want you if you stopped your slaving. You'll identify with what's written here, agree with it, and get excited about doing it all. You may even begin to actually put the Satisfaction Actions to use—until it begins to feel too risky. Under stress (that is, even the remotest possibility that he won't approve of your changing your style on him), you'll be tempted to stop and fall back on what you know so well. You'll want to take up your caretaking again, even though it makes you tired, angry, and disgusted with yourself—because it keeps your man around.

Sandwiched between the multitude of rescuing and caretaking activities that fill your busy days, you have somehow found the time to read this book. So you are well on your way to shedding your exhausting and ineffective love substitute. You, who have toiled, sacrificed, and given above and beyond the call of duty, can stop trying so hard to be your man's needed (and very needy) servant and learn to be his loving and self-empowered partner.

To make that vital transformation you will need to:

ACKNOWLEDGE that you are a Rescuer and then make an honest assessment of how little it has actually benefited *you*. Not only has it left you weary and deathly afraid of losing your indispensability, but it also has made you lose loads of respect for Black men—and for yourself. Don't call your rescuing love, commitment, supportivness, or anything else. Call it what it is: volunteer slavery!

RESIST the idea that the advice in the next section is the recipe for keeping the man in your life so well-tended to that he will stay dependent upon you. Nothing here is meant to help you foster or sustain his dependence on you and your exceptional abilities. The Satisfaction Actions ahead are to assist you in becoming lovingly responsive to your man's needs, not to keep taking responsibility for them. Resist the idea that love is only defined as unlimited caretaking.

EXPECT to feel the emotional effects of withdrawal from your addiction to rescuing and fixing the men in your life. You will battle with guilt and ambivalence as you attempt to apply the principles I will suggest to you. Directly or indirectly, the man in your life is likely to voice his displeasure with your new actions and attitudes, accusing you of suddenly becoming "cold-blooded," "heartless," and "uncaring." Even if he goes so far as to threaten to depart, you must be steadfast in your determination to refrain from your rescuing and caretaking ways. Change may be traumatic for both of you, but that doesn't mean you shouldn't change, and change now.

COMMIT to a love life with a Black man that includes the necessity of sometimes saying *no* and living with the consequences. You are certain to become less indispensable to him, but you will also respect yourself more. You will respect him more too, for letting you have a cherished place in his life without requiring that you be his social worker/baby-sitter/mother/manager and all-around life-support system.

## Avoiders

*Your love life's theme song: "Distant Lover"*

Janice is single and very attractive. She enjoys an active and reasonably happy life—loving parents, good friends, a challenging job, and a beautiful apartment. There are plenty of men in her life. They are Janice's good buddies who love to confide in her, enjoy her crazy sense of humor and her extraordinary cooking skills. They think the world of her, often describing her as:

"a real sweetheart"
"a big help"
"my home girl"
"my running buddy"
"like a sister to me"

A few of Janice's male friends have found themselves romantically attracted to her and wanted to pursue it further. But Janice has a very convincing way of persuading them that a romance would only ruin their friendship. She is masterful at getting them to think that keeping the relationship strictly platonic is their idea. She thinks the guys are great and would be wonderful catches for any woman—except her. Janice is scared to death of romance, because it holds too many possibilities of falling on your face, exposing your heart, and, ultimately, being rejected.

Fran is the chairperson of her church's singles' group. She gets tremendous satisfaction from knowing that her efforts have directly or indirectly brought several couples together, and even resulted in one marriage. The group's biggest event of the year is a Valentine's Day dance for couples only. Fran works feverishly to make sure everyone has a great time. At first several men would ask Fran if they could be her date for the evening. They no longer ask, knowing that Fran will be supervising the food, the music, and even the parking, arguing that she's much too busy seeing to things to be a good date for anyone.

If you're an Avoider you will:

- Only get close enough to men to be their friends—you'll avoid becoming anyone's lover.
- Study men, and the world of romance, but avoid getting involved in it.
- Settle for men's respect and admiration, and avoid their romantic or sexual attraction to you.
- Store up lots of wisdom about the dynamics of satisfying relationships, but avoid any context where you would get to use it.
- Have made an unconscious but committed vow to avoid initiating a relationship with a man, but suppose that when "The One and Only Right One" comes along you will be irresistibly taken over and finally give yourself to love.

Avoiders pitch their tents smack-dab in the middle of Lovers' Lane, but they also build a little fence around it, so that they can watch others' romances unfold around them without fearing any of it might spill over on them. They aren't just afraid of being loved, they don't even see themselves as eligible for love, so they automatically disqualify themselves from its pursuit. Avoiders do, however, see themselves as prime candidates for big-time rejection. If there's any within a hundred miles of her, she is sure it will find her.

For Avoiders, watching others do it, and being near enough to support and advise them in it, is plenty close and cozy enough. Avoiders put on their best satin gowns and go to the ball, but they sit on the sidelines snapping their fingers and tapping their toes while everyone else takes to the dance floor.

Avoiders have hit upon a perfectly danger-free way to have the benefits of close relationships with desirable Black men without taking a chance on the heart-wrenching rejection that they suspect is inevitable in love. They count on these platonic relationships to provide a safe haven right on the periphery of love. So what if I am a little lonely over here, they tell themselves, at least I'm safe.

If you are an Avoider, observing love from a distance is just enough to make you hunger for experiencing it up close. Whether you ever pursue it or not, you will be close enough to smell the enticing aroma of deeply satisfying love, but unless you decide to overcome your fears and take some necessary risks, you will never know the pleasure of tasting it. Observation without participation results in big-time frustration.

## Are You an Avoider?

### *True or false?*

1. You have close male friends who frequently confide in you about their relationships with other women.
2. You have read far more relationship-oriented self-help books, romance novels, or women's magazine articles on love than most of your women friends.
3. You often find other women's concern with makeup, fashion, and hair care to be silly, or "just not for me."
4. You get very self-conscious and tempted to retreat when a man you consider attractive shows some romantic interest in you.
5. You seldom, if ever, date.
6. Other than family, few if any men are ever participants in celebrating your birthday or other personally significant events.
7. You have seldom, or never, found a Black man who met your standards for a potential lover or husband.

8. When you are in social settings with Black men you are much more comfortable talking about them, or others, than about yourself.

9. You have some physical characteristic about which you are self-conscious (such as your weight, your height, your style of speech, a certain facial feature).

10. You are known and respected as a good matchmaker.

11. Your romantic relationships can be described as intense but very brief, or long-term but very shallow.

12. You have felt envy when a man to whom you were attracted, but never allowed close access to you, became involved with someone else.

13. You are in a relationship where your partner disregards you and fails to respond to your most important needs. You hurt deeply, but you are fairly passive.

If you answered true to *any* of these, you have some Avoider tendencies that can, and no doubt already do, hinder your relationships and your life in general. The more times you answered true, the more deeply ingrained and acceptable to you this safety-seeking love substitute has become, and the more it shows up in your style of relating to Black men.

All of the seventy-three Satisfaction Actions to come are for you, but especially those that have the ❱ Avoider symbol above the title. Play closest attention to them, because for you they are the most needed—and the most likely to be denied, resisted, or dismissed.

### YOUR FANTASY RELATIONSHIP

A knight in shining armor will come and beg you to be his. When his begging fails to woo you, he'll sweep you off your feet and carry you away. He'll gladly spend the rest of his life proving how much he must have you, even though you persist in declaring that you can live without him. He will expose his heart to the possibility of your rejection daily, but you will never have to. And so, you will live happily ever after.

YOUR PROBLEM

You feel ineligible for men's love. You are fascinated with them, and truly treasure their presence in your life, but you fear that if you cross the line into romance you will become too vulnerable and they will certainly hurt you. So you have become skilled at keeping men at a safe, comfortable distance. You also have a nagging suspicion that you are just "too" something (unattractive, unromantic, inexperienced) or "not enough" something (interesting, confident, sexy) to measure up to his abiding affection. You are deathly afraid of putting your suspicion to the test, so you seldom, if ever, risk romance. But because you dread being alone, and because you are such a "people person," you get close to men by becoming their ever-present, ever-faithful, nonthreatening, undemanding pal. That way you have a seat right down front to observe all the action without ever getting in the game.

AS YOU READ THIS BOOK

As an Avoider you won't merely read this book. Like the many other self-help books you've read, you will devour it, digest it—to be able to share it with others. You'll find the Satisfaction Actions to be interesting concepts that other women who have relationships should definitely consider applying—and you'll tell them so.

As an Avoider, you are, in many ways, already well-prepared to take the actions that will be suggested to you in the next section of this book. You already love men and, as importantly, you already understand how relationships that work take some work. You are full of energy and you believe in self-improvement. There is, however, one obstacle in your path that threatens to block you from the benefits of loving a Black man. It's the fact that you really can't envision yourself as the much sought after and highly prized object of some desirable Black man's love. And until you begin to see yourself that way, you will continue to avoid the possibility of rejection, and you'll continue to miss out on love, and you'll continue to feel lonely, even with lots of friends around you.

I want to assure you that an intimate and highly satisfying relationship with a Black man is no more out of the question for you than for anyone else. The advice in Part II is designed to help you experience that kind of satisfaction. But to successfully follow through with the recommended behaviors, you will need to grit your teeth, stare down your fears, and decide that now is your time to take the plunge. You can begin to step out of your risk-free, safety-seeking zone and into the exciting challenges and deep satisfaction that await you in romance if you:

ACKNOWLEDGE that your avoiding tendencies have held you captive and severely restricted your life. Your built-in risk-avoiding mechanism will try to convince you that this advice is not for you, and that to attempt it is to court disaster—cruel rejection. You'll be nearly persuaded that you should stop, turn around, and flee to safer ground. If you keep acknowledging that you are an Avoider who has too often talked yourself out of the kind of love you yearn for, it will be easier to ignore the stop signs and boldly choose the way of long-term satisfaction over short-term safety.

RESIST procrastination. The urge to wait for your ideal love to happen by before you start to take action can paralyze you. The principles I will share are best applied once you are already in a romantic relationship with a Black man, not merely a platonic one. Decide to pursue it. In other words, you still have to take the risks before you realize the rewards. Don't wait any longer.

EXPECT, in the words of the old cliché, "to win some and to lose some." For one reason or another, some relationships will prove to be all wrong for one or the other of you. Remember: That doesn't mean men are inherently bad, dangerous, or rejecting of you. It only means that that particular combination didn't work. No lasting harm.

COMMIT to acting "as if." Act as if you are a fearlessly self-assured woman who is interested in and eligible for an intimate relationship with a wonderful man. Act as if men can enrich your life, far more than they can destroy it. These things have every potential of being true in your life, it's just hard for you to believe it. Acting as if is a series of steps of faith that will help transform your vision of yourself.

## Bashers

*Your love life's theme song: "Hit the Road Jack (And Don't You Come Back)"*

Monica met a man who frankly wasn't much to begin with. Lamont was extremely vain and incredibly insensitive. He lost nearly all interest in Monica after their first week together. But for some unknown reason, when he was free (and felt like it) he'd ask Monica out and she'd say yes. Reluctantly, Monica and Lamont became a couple. Neither held much fascination for the other, but they stayed together. Lamont was unfaithful, often broke his promises, and never really was there for Monica when she needed him. On more than one occasion, he was physically abusive to her. Monica and Lamont's relationship has had lots of drama, including several wild public fights. Monica prided herself on her ability to keep Lamont in check with her quick wit and acid tongue. She was an expert at taking verbal jabs at him that always hit just below the belt. The two of them looked more like arch enemies than the lovers they claimed to be. Even though neither Monica nor Lamont got much satisfaction from their relationship, they remained together for over five years.

After their first year Monica thought Lamont was a pretty sorry excuse for a Black man.

After their second year Monica looked around at other Black men and thought she noticed a few Lamont clones.

After their third year Monica began to believe most Black men were as sorry as Lamont.

After their fourth year Monica was convinced that all Black men were more like Lamont than different from him.

After the fifth year Monica determined that Black men are worse than dogs, and her job was to make sure they didn't keep "getting away with it."

Now, seven months after their breakup, Monica has developed a hard-to-shake built-in assumption that the average Black man is only out to exploit and mistreat women. Monica believes she must do it to him before another one gets the chance to do it to her.

Edwina's boyfriend Anton knew that she would go ballistic if he pointed out to Edwina that nearly every time anything goes wrong between them she insists that it's

Anton's fault. To hear her tell it, she is never responsible for having spoken or acted inappropriately toward him. Edwina not only relishes giving Anton a detailed accounting of *what* he supposedly did wrong but usually goes on to tell him his motivations for doing it as well. But what irks Anton more than that is the one time Edwina finally did apologize for a nasty remark she'd made to him, she ended up justifying her behavior, insisting the only reason she made the remark was that Anton knew he had "backed me into a corner."

Bashers are women who expect Black men to be pitiful, and who take responsibility for pointing out their flaws to them and making them pay for them.

If you are a Basher, you deeply resent what you see as the disappointing caliber of available Black men. You feel that you have a just and righteous responsibility to make sure that no man will ever again get half a chance to exploit, reject, abuse, or insult you again. Bashers don't wait long enough to find out if a man is the kind who does exploit. They automatically assume that he is, and then arm themselves for a preemptive attack. Their arsenal? Condemning remarks, toxic attitudes, and ice-cold payback tactics.

Bashing has great appeal because it has anger and indignation at its core. Anger feels very powerful—especially when you feel very weak. Lashing out, setting straight, or paying back a Black man can help you forget that your heart was vulnerable to him in the first place. When you are angry you feel strong and therefore safe.

But being a Basher also has some serious drawbacks. Not the least of which is that it does little to respond to the part of you that used to have some hope and desire for a rich, satisfying relationship. To Bashers, hope feels too much like vulnerability, so you cut it off, push it down, or explain it away. Your personal vision for love dies. In addition, Bashers are so passionate in their pursuit of justice that they will find it very easy to go overboard. In trying to make right every wrong and punish every injustice committed by a guilty man, if you are a Basher you may start doing it not just with men who are guilty as sin, but innocent ones as well. But once they feel the heat of your wrath, they will respond in kind, matching you insult for insult, blow for blow. That's when you will conclude that your low opinion of Black men was right from the outset. Your bashing can trigger the very behavior from him that you hate most. Bashing sets you up for poor treatment.

Bashers:

- Find relationships with Black men to be like competitions with an opponent who *must* be held in check.
- Feel justified and vindicated when they believe their efforts to humble their man by putting him in his place have succeeded.
- Have difficulty accepting any responsibility for the failures of their relationships.
- Resent it when men are turned off by them, but are suspicious when men are attracted to them.
- Have absolutely no patience with disappointments or tears—especially their own.

## Are You a Basher?

### *True or false?*

1. You get a secret jolt of satisfaction when another woman agrees with your sharp criticisms of Black men, or laughs at your disparaging remarks.
2. There is a particular Black man who you believe has owed you a major apology for some time.
3. Something about the title of this book doesn't sit right with you.
4. You sometimes daydream about conflict situations where you are successful in putting a man "in his place."
5. You get a kick out of pointing out how some man made a fool of himself.
6. You require men to jump through hoops to befriend you, hoops that you don't require of women.
7. You have found it hard to contain negative feelings toward a certain Black man because he reminds you of another one from your past.
8. You frequently find yourself challenging male authority figures, feeling compelled to inform them what you "won't take."

9. You strongly believe that men mostly don't have a clue as to how to act in a relationship, and that most women definitely do.
10. A number of times men have asked you to "lighten up" or "give me a break" or "chill out" in response to your style of relating to them.
11. You sometimes catch yourself rehearsing in your mind long detailed scripts where you are catching, confronting, and chastising some erring Black man.
12. Your closest male friends are either homosexual, married, or in some way at a lower level than you. It is clear that you stand above them in some way.
13. You are aware of feeling very angry about this test.

If you answered true to *any* of these, you have some Basher tendencies that can, and no doubt already do, hinder your relationships and your life in general. The more times you answered true, the more deeply ingrained and acceptable to you this safety-seeking love substitute has become, and the more it shows up in your style of relating to Black men.

All of the seventy-three Satisfaction Actions to come are for you, but especially those that have the ■ Basher symbol above the title. Play closest attention to them, because for you they are the most needed—and the most likely to be denied, resisted, or dismissed.

### YOUR FANTASY RELATIONSHIP

You'd be with a humble, apologetic man who was just intimidated enough by you to give you respect and reverence, but not the kind of respect that comes from a loving partner, rather that which comes from a semireformed convict to his parole officer. You really want him to be, at least a little, scared of you and the awesome power you wield.

### YOUR PROBLEM

Incredible rage. Your seething anger over the accumulation of real or supposed slights, unkindnesses, and demeaning acts from some Black men has now spilled over onto all of them. Your rage makes you feel powerful, and power makes you feel safe and secure. So being enraged is very important to you. By bashing you get the momentary satisfaction of justice being served, but you never find the long-lasting satisfaction that comes from relationships of intimacy, mutual approval, and respect.

### As You Read This Book

You are probably tempted not to read this book at all. You are pretty sure already that this is pro-male, anti-female tripe that can't possibly mean you any good. You will be tempted to read things into the Satisfaction Actions that support your point of view, because taking deliberate actions that may benefit a Black man feels too much like it's disregarding you. You will have difficulty benefiting from this book unless you commit to an attitude adjustment.

But if you keep reading with an open mind, and even a teaspoon of willingness to try a different approach to relating to men, you may soon find yourself trading in some of your anger for some genuine joy. It's not too late for you, or for him. It's not too late for you and him together. You've tried it your way, and though bashing helps you feel like you're a winner and he's a loser, it's a lonely, bitter, and ultimately unsatisfying victory. If you know deep within that you would still like more out of love, then I'm challenging you to use the upcoming Satisfaction Actions to help you get it.

Of course some men *are* no good. Not for you, or anyone else. Hold on. Don't jump to any hasty conclusions, but if your partner is abusive or consistently proves hazardous to your physical, mental, or emotional health, no actions you take will be enough to turn him around. In that case you help neither him nor yourself by sticking around for it. Removing yourself from his destructive presence is a legitimate option; returning the abuse isn't. To get the fullest benefit from the love lessons in Part II you will find it helpful to begin to do the following now:

ACKNOWLEDGE that you have definite Basher tendencies. It will be impossible to stay motivated to work through the upcoming principles if you are not honest about the need for change.

RESIST (at least for the time being) everything you say or do with Black men that is designed to correct an injustice. Determine to stop working so much overtime in judging, critiquing, and paying them back. It may feel to you like the whole world will fall apart if you don't continue your crusade. Let it.

EXPECT men to continue to exhibit some of the faults, flaws, and imperfections that you loathe so much, but look for the good. Work to get back in touch with men's positive, desirable, and highly appealing characteristics. Even if you find them to be few, look for them. Don't require men to earn your loving use of the behaviors I will suggest ahead; give them freely. Do it not merely for his sake, but for yours too, and for the sake of your freedom from the bondage of your rage and excessive mistrust.

COMMIT to trying these principles in spite of your feelings. Don't let your emotions be your guide. They are too heavily stacked in favor of your love substitute already. Don't wait until you feel like doing what will be suggested to you, do it until you feel like doing it. Then do it some more. More simply, you may have to "fake it till you make it."

# It's Time for
# a Change

The pages ahead contain seventy-three straightforward and uncomplicated but highly effective ways to love a Black man. Some of what you will find may seem like "old news," and you'll be very proud of how well you already know and do them. Give them your attention anyway, as they will be useful reminders, helping you to troubleshoot your weak areas and blind spots. Then keep reading and you will encounter others that will speak profoundly to you and your situation, inspiring you to learn and live what is truly effective in loving a Black man, with more understanding and more courage, and ultimately, more satisfaction.

Don't just analyze and memorize these Satisfaction Actions—perform them. The most effective way to break old useless habits is to replace them with new, more rewarding ones. These can radically alter the way you and the man in your life experience love. To adopt even a handful of the directives ahead will make a dramatic difference. To adopt most, or all, of them will revolutionize your love life, and not coincidentally transform you personally.

But what will happen to your need to feel safe and secure in love, out of harm's way, and no longer subject to the quirks, idiosyncracies, whims, and mysterious nature of men? Are there any guarantees that loving a Black man in the ways suggested here will keep you from ever again feeling the dazed confusion, bitter rejection, awkwardness, and the frustration and disappointment you have experienced in the past?

You can have love, but you can't have guarantees. Love involves another person, and whenever there is another person involved in anything, the idea of guarantees becomes irrelevant. You don't have control over how he will act and how much or how little he will fit your definition of who and how he should be. What you do have control over is you. You can make a decision to cease your preoccupation with the pursuit of your own safety and comfort and make a choice to pursue risky, exhilarating, soul-stirring, heartwarming love with the Black man already in your life, or one who's on the way.

# The Satisfaction Actions and You

Give yourself time to carefully read and digest the information and suggestions given for each Satisfaction Action. Pay closest attention to the ones that have your love substitute's symbol at the top.

A brief personal statement precedes each of these seventy-three actions. None of them are the exact words of any one woman (the names under each represent the composite stories of many women). The statements are, however, experiences and comments typical of what women who love Black men have shared with me in private counseling, on the radio, and elsewhere.

At the end of each of the Satisfaction Actions are two special features. "Say it" provides a brief affirmation that encapsulizes and reinforces what you have read. Repeat each of them aloud as you read through. Continue to do so daily as you work to adopt the Satisfaction Actions that most apply to you. The affirmations will help prepare your mind and nudge your will into taking the suggested actions.

Of even greater importance is the "Do it" feature. This will challenge you to turn the principles into practice, by suggesting an immediately doable action in response to the insights you will have just read. Developing or sharpening positive habits requires taking the steps, not just reading about them.

So shake off your fears, put away your reservations, beg, borrow, or steal some courage and *do*—and keep doing—the Satisfaction Actions suggested ahead. To do so you must only be willing. Don't wait until you are ready and able, being willing is enough to start.

# PART II

# How to Love a Black Man

# 1. ▲ ■ ● ◆ ◗
## *Expect Black Men to Be Very Different from the Women Who Love Them*

*"Before I started going out with Derek, I used to complain about only having my girlfriends to talk to and spend time with. I got so tired of women's voices, women's conversations, women's ways of looking at things. It was too predictable, too familiar. I've been with Derek for about six months now, and I swear, men and women are from two different worlds. Dealing with men and trying to understand where they are coming from may be a lot of things, but it is definitely* not *predictable or familiar."*

*—Johnetta*

Black men are different from you. The differences are not defects or dysfunction, though—everybody has those. They are just differences. Some of them are significant, and in a relationship they are so close up and in your face that you're bound to notice them, and maybe to dread them too.

Genetics, history, and his upbringing have all conspired to make his "he-ness" vastly different from your "she-ness." If these differences are not understood they can seriously frustrate the woman who loves Black men. If they are understood, they can constantly fascinate her.

- He is different from you in how he perceives the world.
- He is different from you in how he processes and expresses his emotions.
- He is different from you in how he is motivated.
- He is different from you in how he talks and how he hears.
- He is different from you in what he values and what he does.
- He is different from you in how he relates in love and romance.

One of the most hazardous mistakes you can make is to use what you understand about yourself (in particular) or womankind (in general) to try to make sense of Black mankind. That's like trying to understand the sun by studying the moon. They are not the same. It's not good for the health of your relationship with him. It's definitely not good for your mental health either.

Noticing the differences can often amuse you, and sometimes annoy you. But don't be intimidated by them. Every day expect him to show you, in many ways, just how different Adam is from Eve. You needn't be overwhelmed by this curious fact of nature. Once you accept the fundamental differences you can certainly handle them.

Why, you ask, is he so incredibly, frustratingly, mysteriously, outlandishly different? Why ask why? The time and energy you spend pondering that cosmic question could be used more productively elsewhere, like in discovering and appreciating the differences, instead of resenting them, or worse yet, trying to make them all go away.

Accept, even embrace, the differences and get on with your love life together. Drop out of the useless "no credit" course in "Why?" and go for your Ph.D. in "How?"—to love a Black man. (You actually signed up for it the moment you began reading this book.)

**Say it:** "I acknowledge that Black men are different from me, and the differences are often mysterious. I can learn to appreciate, not just tolerate, those differences. The man I love is no failure when he fails to be like me."

**Do it:** Enlist three men you truly respect (for example, your father, lover, husband, minister). Invite them to lunch, individually or together. Discuss together the significant differences you perceive between the characteristics of men and the women who love them. Examine both the internal and external differences. Ask their opinions about what helps bridge the gaps and what doesn't. Share your findings with three sister-friends you truly respect.

# 2. ▲■ *Don't Get All Your Knowledge of Black Men from Women*

*"I remember when* Jungle Fever *came out. I called three of my close girlfriends and we rushed out to see it. All of us loved Spike Lee movies and we had heard a lot about this one in particular. So there we were, these four women who talk about anything and everything together—especially men. We were munching on popcorn and caught up in the action when that scene came on. You know, the one where all the sisters are sitting around in a circle philosophizing about how Black men act in relationships. All four of us turned and looked at each other there in the dark—and we all knew why. We saw ourselves up on that screen and heard some of the exact same things that we had said to each other. It was too funny."*

*—Akita*

It is absolutely essential that the object of your love is also the subject of your comprehensive research and investigation. Knowing what you know about Black men—your Black man in particular—shouldn't be the result of looking to just one authoritative source—other women. Don't fail to find out about men from men.

Your perspectives on the male animal should, of course, be seasoned by observation, common sense, and personal experience—your own and that of others. But the real substance of your understanding of men shouldn't be limited to the findings, opinions, and analyses of female "experts" only. What do men teach you themselves?

Other women, well intentioned though they may be, cannot tell you the whole story. They can tell you what they perceive, suspect, assume, hope, and believe based on personal experience—or lack thereof. They can tell you Black men do this, say that, think or need or want or feel this or that or the other. They cannot, however, tell you exactly what these things mean about men. And, ultimately, isn't that what you need to know?

If stones could talk, asking the Rock of Gibraltar, or even a tiny pebble on the beach, to tell you about itself would be far more enlightening than volumes of scientific observations from outside experts. Each rock could recount its evolution to you and explain how and why it possesses hard spots and soft ones, smooth surfaces and jagged edges. They could tell you their own stories.

Throughout your entire relationships career you will be busy gathering data and drawing conclusions based on that data. Don't let other women's input on men, based on good times or bad, be all you have to draw upon. Ask men about men. Learn men from men.

**Say it:** "I have not heard the whole story about Black men until I have listened to Black men tell it. My sisters and I are indeed the experts on how we feel and what we think about men, nothing more, but nothing less either."

**Do it:** Complete this sentence: "In romantic relationships, Black men are _____." Do your responses in the form of a list. Ask yourself, where did I get each of these beliefs? From women only? Men only? A balanced blend of the two? Based on your honest answers and insights from this section, how much, or how little, can you rely on your beliefs?

# 3. ■ ◆ *Resist Comparisons*

*"I couldn't wait to take him with me to my church on Sunday. I knew that if he could just see my minister one time he would immediately see why I always say the two of them look, act, and talk so much alike you'd think they were clones. I meant it as a compliment. Reverend Dawson was up speaking when we came in. As soon as we slid into our pew, I looked over at Greg and said, 'Now look at him. Don't you look just like—' Before I could get it out, Greg cut me off and said, 'Celeste, your minister looks like your minister, and I look like me. Okay?' I could tell that for whatever the reason, that was the last he wanted to hear about that."*

*—Celeste*

"You're just like . . ." These three little words, and all their cousins, seem so well-meaning and totally lacking in the ability to harm, but be advised, they are dangerous and capable of inflicting great pain. Thou shalt not compare a Black man to anyone, living or dead, famous or infamous, good or bad.

Comparisons are so appealing. They add color and clarity to your conversation, allowing you to make your point concisely and vividly: "My previous boyfriend/husband/lover didn't do it/say it/see it/like it like that . . ." Or "You look just like . . ." Or (recognize this one?) "Why can't you be like . . . ?" But work harder to communicate the essence of what you're saying another way.

When you compare a Black man to any other man, you are contrasting him with some preconceived standard of excellence—or ridiculousness. Using comparisons will eat away at his prized sense of individuality and undermine your efforts to affirm his uniqueness. Comparisons make it seem as though he's only as good as So-and-So, or as rotten as Such-and-Such. Treasuring his individuality the way he does, he is likely to hear it as a demand to be more like What's-His-Name or less like Whatchamacallit. Men place a high value on the freedom to be like themselves and no other. Your man relishes the assurance that, on his own terms, he is marvelously acceptable to you.

Strangely, a Black man may compare himself to others, and be just fine about it. In this way men do their personal troubleshooting and get themselves back on line. You can't afford to join them at it, however, for by doing so, you can too easily offend, trigger his flight mechanism, and tempt him to take off. He'll feel burdened with trying to live up to someone else's identity, or trying to avoid the humiliation of failing to live up to it.

If you must do some comparing, let it be a contrast between who your man is now and who you believe your man has every potential of becoming, or who he used to be. Compare him to himself and no one else.

**Say it:** "I can compare things with things, but never a Black man with any other man. I will make the effort to commend or confront elements of his uniqueness without relying on comparisons. I will resist."

**Do it:** Make a mental note to red-flag yourself whenever you use the phrase "just like" in reference to your mate. Back up and make your point to him another way, comparison-free.

# 4. ■ ◆ Expect to Be Treated Well Rather Than Badly

*"No, I don't need him to always be opening and closing the car door for me, and laying his jacket down over puddles for me to walk over. All that's cute, but that's not what I'm talking about. I'm talking about real basic stuff like showing up somewhere near the time he said he would, and coming to my door, instead of*

*blowing from the curb, and, oh yeah . . . not trying to get some other woman's*
*phone number while he's out with me. I'm not expecting to be treated like a diva*
*or something, but come on now. After dealing with guys who just don't seem to*
*have a clue how to treat a woman, it's like uh-oh here comes another caveman!"*

—*Natalie*

How a man treats you reveals a great deal about the quality of that man. Your expectations of him can have a powerful effect on his treatment of you. The higher your genuine and realistic expectations of him, the more likely he is to meet them. No, I'm not talking about some magical abracadabra maneuvers, and I am not trying to convince you that whatever you envision you'll get. Life doesn't work that way. But expecting and appreciating good treatment from your man will help you keep getting it.

You may be surprised to know that according to recent official census statistics: "Most Black men are *not* dogs." Sure, you've known some with canine characteristics—they bark loudly, they want their appetites to be served immediately, and they generally make a mess of things. But those Fidos are the exceptions—not the norm.

Black men, in general, are capable of treating you with the well-mannered sensitivity and dignity you desire and deserve. You create a climate for that kind of treatment when you go in expecting it. It's best when his treatment of you can be described as gentlemanly and gracious; and you show appreciation, but not surprise.

It's the kind of attitude that says to a man, "I invite you to show me your best, and I'll be terribly surprised should you show me any less." It springs from your predetermined faith in how well he can treat you, rather than preconceived notions as to how well he won't treat you.

Faith in him is not the same as helpless dependence upon him to give you something you can't get for yourself. In the final analysis, you are responsible for treating yourself very well. You give the man in your life the opportunity to join you in that responsibility.

**Say it:** "My low-level expectations of him can leave him satisfied with low-level performance. My (realistically) high-level expectations encourage his high-level performance."

**Do it:** List at least five actual verbal and nonverbal ways you can effectively communicate your high expectations of your man's treatment of you. Incorporate them immediately into your dealings with him.

# 5. ▲▶ *Study Other Women Who Love Black Men Well*

*"There are some things that I can always count on—they just never change. One is our entire family getting together at one of our homes for Thanksgiving dinner. That's when I can always count on all the men to eventually gravitate to one part of the house—usually the room with the TV or the pool table—and all the women to another—usually the kitchen. All of the women surrender the old husbands or new boyfriends to play dominoes, watch football, crack jokes about us, or whatever it is men do on these occasions. Another thing I can always count on is coming in to call the men to dinner and finding my cousin Velma right in the middle of them—and having a ball. She's famous for that. They all love to have her around and she looks right at home with them. Every year we tease her about hanging out with the men. Her standard comeback is: 'Honey, you know me. Show me where the men are, and I'll show you where the fun is.' "*

*—Sharon*

One of the best things you could ever do for yourself in learning to love a Black man is to take serious note of the woman who already does it exceptionally well. She's your sister who knows how to be a friend to men, not just a lover, but a full-time, all-out, dyed-in-the-wool friend. Learn from her.

Women who comfortably relate to Black men have a powerful gift. Men see them a mile off and are magnetically drawn to them. Other women see them and greatly admire or intensely envy them. Watch her closely and you will observe her "man-friendly" gift reflected in the easygoing, right-at-home way she is with men. She is comfortable enough to throw her head back and laugh with them; and she instinctively knows when laughter is out of place and confrontation, debate, or even departure are in order.

She's no phony. She has no need for men's approval. She appreciates and accommodates all that makes men different from women, without trying to be one of the boys. She loves men, but without a doubt she genuinely *likes* them too.

What is she doing that causes her, and the man she's with, to be so comfortable in their own skin? There are valuable lessons to learn from her about the kind of self-confidence and simplicity that allow her to welcome the opposite sex rather than put up a NO TRESPASSING sign.

She is accessible to men because she's not afraid of them. She genuinely enjoys their company, and is secure enough to show it. She speaks to them confidently and listens attentively. She knows how to double over with laughter with a man—but never at his expense. She takes seriously what he does—because he does.

If you know one such as she, follow her, study her. Don't get hung up on how old or young, or plain or fancy she may be. Learn from her. If you are one, look with care all around you. Some sister, or several, may be watching you. Teach her right. And, on behalf of Black men everywhere, thank you very much.

**Say it:** "I have as much ability as any woman to put up an invisible welcome sign for men. 'True sister available here.' I will study others who do it well. I will do as they do."

**Do it:** Identify the most self-assured, confident, and "man-friendly" woman you know. Closely study her style of interacting with the Black men in her life. Take special note of her tone, conversation, and whatever else that demonstrates her warmth and openness to men. Use her model to make necessary changes in your style of relating with the man in your life.

# 6. ▲ ● ◆ *Never Compromise on Your Principles— Do Compromise on Your Practices*

*"I have pretty much decided that I have gotten too grown to start breaking some of my personal rules to live by, just to please a man. I feel like I've already done enough giving in and compromising on what really mattered to me to last a lifetime. In the couple of months we've been together, I have sometimes noticed Everett trying to get me to change my mind about something important to me. He was determined we were going to spend the weekend together at his boss's cabin up in the mountains. I do not feel comfortable with us shacking up together over any weekends. I thanked him for inviting me, and said no, and even explained why the idea was unacceptable to me. Everett kept trying to persuade me. He just wouldn't quit. Finally I said, 'Everett, nothing is going to change my mind on this, so would you please drop it?' Knowing Everett though, when I get home there'll be a message from him on my machine, telling what time he plans to pick me up Friday to head to the mountains."*

*—Ethel*

When you too easily abandon your own principles, you lack integrity. When you refuse to compromise on the way you *practice* your principles, you lack flexibility. Both lack of integrity and lack of flexibility work against a loving relationship with a Black man.

Your principles are the morals and values that guide and govern your life. They are not so much about what you do, or how you do things. They are, very simply, about what you believe is right and wrong. They are your personal "nonnegotiables" for which you cannot sit down, shut up, or back off. For them you must take courage and stand your ground.

Your principles are as much representative of who you are as your fingerprints, your DNA, and your image in the mirror. When you compromise them you play the role of a woman who has a different set of values than yours. It's an acting job for which you win no Oscar and receive no pay in a drama that never has a happy ending.

Flexibility, negotiation, and compromise are at the heart of loving relationships. Without them no real common ground can ever be established. An unwillingness to compromise on your practices, the way you do a thing in light of your principles, is rigid inflexibility. Actually, there are a million ways to do a thing right. In loving someone you must willingly and frequently employ negotiation and compromise to find common ground and make corporate decisions with your partner. It is the only way two very different human beings can live lovingly together.

Finding a way to compromise on how you put your principles into practice requires creativity, humility, and unwavering appreciation for each other's values. To allow for alteration of the way you do a thing is not only possible, it's crucial. It speaks highly of your commitment to join in making life choices that will work for both of you, without violating the principles of either of you.

**Say it:** "I must keep a tight focus on the principles that define who I am, and what I hold to be right. That's the integrity part of me. Since there is more than one way to do anything, I must remain open to compromising my way for us to discover our way. That's the flexibility part of me."

**Do it:** Write a list of what you consider to be some of the uncompromisable moral laws you live by. How might you uphold them, and at the same time be appropriately flexible in the practice of them with the man in your life?

# 7. ▲● *Demand Respect—Model Self-Respect*

*"I laughed because it really was funny, but in a sick, disgusting kind of way. Jerome and I went to this very trendy, supposed-to-be chic club downtown to celebrate our anniversary. All night long there's this woman, who had obviously had way too much to drink, making a fool of herself. She loud-talked the man she was with and started grabbing other guys on the dance floor, demanding they dance with her. She was so obnoxious and she was getting on everybody's nerves. Eventually Girlfriend came over and attached herself to this guy near us—who was already dancing with somebody else! She stepped right in, trying to do the Bump, or some crazy drunken version of it, with him. Well one time she must have bumped a little too hard, because she lost her balance and hit the floor with a splat. Her wig went one way and she went another! That was it. Everybody in the place fell out laughing. Security came and shoveled her up and escorted her to the exit. The funny part was, as she left hobbling on a shoe whose heel had come off, Girlfriend had the nerve to yell at the security guard: 'Take your hands off of me. Don't you know how to show some respect to a lady?' "*

*—Tanya*

Respect isn't like parking tickets or taxes—nobody can be *made* to pay it. Request respect from where you want it and remove yourself from where you don't get it. You can only do that when you already have your self-respect.

Respecting you is not the same as bowing down in worship before you. To respect you is to acknowledge your significance as a human being of the female variety and in every way to treat you accordingly. Respect is due you simply because you *are*.

Before you demand respect from others, you'll do well to already possess an accurate appraisal of your own self-worth and constantly demonstrate how much you believe it. Self-respect means treating yourself like a class act and accepting no less than that from others. You do that by the dignified way you carry yourself, the confidence and discretion in your speech and manner, and the obvious finesse with which you move toward people who respect you, and away from those who don't.

Men give you respect in direct proportion to the level of respect you show for yourself. If you have much, he is likely to show much. If you have a little, he'll show a little. If you have none, he'll certainly match it. You have the power to help him discover that if it walks like a lady, talks like a lady, looks and acts like a lady, it is one . . . and she must be treated, in all ways, like one.

**Say it:** "I don't become a woman of worth just when he treats me like one. I already am one and treat myself as one. I invite him to add his respect for me, to my respect for myself."

**Do it:** Individually share this chapter with at least one woman and one man you know very well. Ask their honest opinions on how well or how poorly you command respect from men and demonstrate self-respect. Ask them to describe some of your specific behavior patterns that need to be adjusted. (Note: If both friends point out some of the same things, count on those being worthy of your immediate attention.)

# 8. ▲ ●
# *Let What You Say and What You Mean Be the Same*

*"I guess I really need to work on being more straightforward or something. As it is now, Anthony says he can always tell where I'm coming from by believing I meant the*

*opposite of what I said. I don't think it's all that bad, but I did catch myself last week trying to convince him that I didn't mind at all if he went skiing without me. I gave him all this B.S. about how he probably needed some time to himself and I was just fine about it. Then, when he got back, I jumped all over him for actually doing it."*

*—Brittany*

Men are generally more literal-minded than women. They can appreciate symbolism, suggestion, and subtlety, but your best bet with a Black man is to say exactly what you mean, the way you mean it. Then he can get busy responding to what you really meant, rather than what he may only *think* you meant.

Whenever you open your mouth to send a message to the man in your life, expect him to believe you mean what you say. You make knowing and understanding you much easier when you say what you mean and mean what you say in the first place. Do it, and you'll find out that the risk of confusion and misunderstanding is automatically and dramatically reduced.

It's a simple point, but full of practical value in the business of relating to a Black man: If you say it, mean it. If you don't, don't. Sending mixed messages with a little yes, a little no, and a little maybe in them will eventually leave at least one of you with tight jaws and hurt feelings.

Don't say: "Whatever you decide is all right with me ..." when what you really mean is: "I'm counting on you to make a decision based on what you know I want."

Don't say: "I've got a million things to do tonight. We'll have to play it by ear about getting together ..." when what you really mean is: "I feel like being alone tonight. We'll have to get together another time."

Don't say: "That's okay; it didn't matter ..." when what you really mean is: "That will be the last time you will ever do that to me!"

You may be quite surprised at how offended he *doesn't* get when you offer him the pure, buck-naked what's on your mind. You needn't be rude or insensitive; just honestly and consistently say what you mean.

**Say it:** "The world's greatest authority on what I'm thinking, feeling, or meaning is me. For him to know what I really mean, requires that I say it and mean it when I do."

**Do it:** Spend the day with a friend or lover. Tell him you are determined to practice saying exactly what you mean the entire time. Ask your companion to check you and challenge you to shoot straight and avoid confusing double-talk. At the end of the day grade yourself, and get a grade from your companion.

# 9. ■ ◆ *Disagree, Agreeably*

*"Sometimes I get turned off by all the love and marriage books and tapes that try to make it seem like every argument a couple has should be done with that lovey-dovey, mild-mannered tone. I call it picnic talk—like asking your man for more champagne or something. Please . . . ! Try that with a Black man and see how far you get. I know loud talk and going off may not be the best way to go—but you have to be real."*

*—Sylvia*

It takes little to no effort to feel close and content in a relationship with a man with whom you always agree. Perhaps you believe in the old compatibility cliché, which argues that two people who love each other will undoubtedly agree with each other. It's faulty mathematics that assumes that 1 man in love + 1 woman in love = 1 opinion on all matters. The numbers just don't add up.

Finding that the two of you disagree on some things is not necessarily a crisis. However, finding that your disagreements are dealt with destructively is. Agreeable disagreement is vital to success in loving a Black man.

Men actually find disagreements to be like a challenging little jigsaw puzzle, strewn in a thousand pieces, and begging to be put together. They are fascinated with the logical, rational, and factual, and they love the art of persuasion. To men, a disagreement is their opportunity to perform the deeply satisfying tasks of presenting, clarifying, and arguing their points.

Black men admire and pursue excellence in performance. For them, even conflicts and arguments are cherished opportunities to perform a tricky task—and to succeed at it. For you to know that, and to not take it too personally when he differs with you, makes it possible for you to disagree quite agreeably.

Disagreements between yourselves need not descend into missile-launching theatrics. It is not important that one of you goes away with a big "I Was Right You Were Wrong" trophy. Neither should a disagreement become a signal to shut up, shut down, and shut out your partner, in order to keep the peace.

If your man goes away feeling like he's bad, wrong, or undeniably low-down because he disagreed with you, he won't be able to bear listening to you and affirming you and your right to hold an opinion contrary to his. Let him know it's okay for him to disagree (agreeably) with you.

Disagreements that get ugly hinder both of you from getting what you need from each other. To make your disagreements more agreeable:

- Maintain an agreeable tone of voice (neither screaming nor sweet-toned sarcasm are useful).
- Speak with agreeable body language. Adjust your physical presence so that it conveys "I'm here and I'm hearing you" messages.
- Remember that making your point doesn't require that you destroy his, and listening to his doesn't mean losing yours.
- Start with the assumption that when he shares his personal opinion with you, he is not making a personal attack on you. (When he is, bring to his attention what you perceive as attack behavior—not attitude, motives, or other inconclusive nonobservables.)
- Don't require a neat and tidy resolution of every disagreement. One of the marks of a truly grown-up relationship of two mutually respecting partners is the ability to live peaceably with each other's differences of opinion. Be willing to agree to disagree, and leave it like that sometimes.

**Say it:** "I erase disagreement with the man I love from the list of my biggest fears. Every disagreement between my man and me is a great opportunity to send each other a message about what we each value and believe."

**Do it:** Talk to a Black man with whom you are close and have previously had a disagreement. Give each other feedback about what did and didn't work when you talked it out. Try to discover what specific changes in your personal style you can and should make.

# 10. ▲▸ *Follow Through*

*"Gerard and I both agreed that our marriage counseling had been very helpful. We learned so much about each other's fears and hang-ups and where they come from, which was good to know. As long as our therapist was showing us how our childhood experiences and our different personality types were part of the problem, we were fascinated. We were enjoying the whole process then. I think both of us got tense when Dr. Levy started talking about us committing to some concrete changes in how we talk to each other and how we handle our money. Her ideas were good, and doing what she suggested would probably help a lot. But I think Gerard and I were afraid that we'd do what we've done so many times in the past. We'd make big promises to change our ways, then never get around to doing it."*

*—Antoinette*

The easiest thing in the world is to have a great idea, a workable plan, or a surefire strategy for making love work with a Black man. To actually work the plan is a whole 'nother story. The doing of a thing is what takes discipline, effort, and fearlessness. It takes follow-through.

You may have secretly convinced yourself that to never follow through means you can never really fail at your plan. Actually, to never try is to fail.

In loving a Black man, one of your most powerful character traits will be your demonstrated ability to follow through. To look carefully at what it takes on your end to make your relationships work, to commit to the work involved, and then to do it. As you read the Satisfaction Actions in this book, agreeing with their principles is easy. Rising to their challenge, harder. It can be done, but only if you put some motion to your emotions.

Men are much more skilled in reading actions than intentions. They have great appreciation, even admiration, for the thinking, feeling, and planning that leads to *doing*. He values that in himself as well as others.

Follow-through has some formidable opponents, including (but certainly not limited to) distraction, procrastination, and excessive analysis. They scream loudly, tempting you to be a woman who intends to do, rather than one who actually does. You know actions speak louder than words, so focus on your vision for your love life with the Black man you love, and follow through.

**Say it:** "I shall not be content with my own good intentions. Both life and love require action. I can and will follow through."

**Do it:** Which love Satisfaction Action have you read, so far, that you most intend to act on? Pause for a moment. Consider what the steps are you must take to execute it. Even if it will feel like a big inconvenience, follow through on it now.

# 11. ▲ ● ◆ Avoid All Game-Playing and Hidden Agendas

*"My mother and father are so funny together. They've been married almost forty years and you'd swear they are the most well-matched, easygoing couple you'd ever met. They never argue. Most people think they agree about everything. I know different. My mother is from the old school. She tells my father whatever it is she thinks he wants to hear. Then she turns around and does whatever she wants to do. She cons and flatters him to death. I think my mother is dead serious when she*

*laughs behind Daddy's back and says 'Make a man think he's king, and he won't even notice that it's the queen running everything.' "*

*—Anita*

The maxim "deeds done in the dark will always come to the light" is true enough of the times to make it well worth paying attention to. Every woman who will ever love a Black man needs to pay attention to it with her whole heart. Game-playing, hidden agendas, and the manipulation at the core of both never work to produce or sustain real love.

Game-playing involves the calculated use of half-truths, false fronts, and sleight-of-hand in an attempt to produce certain desired outcomes in a relationship. Simply put, it's craftily influencing your lover to feel, think, or act a certain way in order to get your way. It is equal measures of creative genius and downright self-centeredness. Game-playing is the attempt to "get over" on another somebody. Sadly, it's the somebody you say you love.

Hidden agendas are the secret motives that cause one's manipulation muscles to flex in the first place. Hidden agendas are all about what you really want—but don't want to say you want. They are the private, fiercely pursued objectives for which you are willing to do anything to ensure they are met. Game-playing is the means by which the hidden agenda is accomplished:

Hidden Agenda:
"I want to make him regret breaking off with me."
Game played:
"I'll make him jealous, letting him see me out with his friend."
Hidden Agenda:
"I want him to propose marriage to me."
Game played:
"I'll play wife now. I will do his laundry, fix his meals, and follow his lead."
Hidden Agenda:
"I want to break up with him and move on."

Game played:
"I'll play busy, never returning his calls and never available to see him."

Sexual games, money games, power games—one is as bad as the next. Hidden agendas drive up the back roads, sneak over the back fence, and enter through the back door. These are the motives and methods of one who is too frightened or too selfish to be up-front with the man she loves.

Men despise games being played on them and hidden agendas being served on them (even if they are game players and hidden agenda keepers themselves). It makes them feel they are being "worked," and when he feels he's being worked, he also feels he's being stupid. Stupid he hates, and he won't let himself stay that way very long.

When it's all said and done, hidden agendas and games are manifestations of a deep-seated need to be in control of people, situations, or results. Yet it involves a gut-level fear of letting the man you love see you as a Controller. Fear zaps the life out of love and leaves the two of you alone and isolated. You really can't control all of life, so don't try. Control, manipulation, and game-playing are desperate attempts to rule the world of love. You can't.

**Say it:** "I will expose my goals and objectives to the man in my life. I will be up-front, out front, and down front as I learn to accept and live life on life's terms with no games or hidden agendas."

**Do it:** If you were promised, for the next twenty-four hours, $100,000 for every secret agenda you confessed and every manipulative game you abandoned in your relationships, what would it take for you to be a millionaire? Now do it for free.

# 12. *Confront Selfishness—Yours and His*

*"I am no spoiled brat who has to have her way in everything. I just don't see myself as someone who's always looking out for number one and caring little*

*about my husband's feelings and needs. Actually, I'm the one who's always jumping on other women about being so selfish, trying to get without giving much in the relationship. I make long speeches abut how love means looking out for him and not just yourself—and how self-centered women give us all a bad name. I'm all fire and brimstone about that. The other day on the radio, some psychologist said that the character defect that drives us the craziest in others is usually the one that we feel most guilty of ourselves. She said it's easier to condemn others for what we hate about ourselves. I immediately thought: Humh . . . me, selfish?"*

*—Loretta*

Your greatest enemy in love is selfishness. Beware, the enemy is cunning, persistent, and lurks threateningly in your heart and in the heart of the Black man you love.

Selfishness wants what it wants, how it wants it, when it wants it. When you put selfish desire above the needs of the one you love, your enemy is victorious. Keep your eyes open. Selfishness rears its ugly head when you least expect it.

If you see your relationship as first and foremost a place for your needs to be met, your desires to be satisfied, your plans to be realized, your feelings heeded, and your pleasure gained, you've got a selfishness problem.

Confront your selfishness. Deny it the gentle handling and limitless tolerance you have sometimes allowed it in the past. Face its ugliness head-on, call it by name, and evict it from the premises. Selfishness doesn't deserve residence in your life, and certainly not in your love.

Phrases like "I'm trying to find myself some true happiness . . ." sound harmless enough, even commendable. In reality, when sentiments like these top your list of priorities, you've stepped over into the Land of Me, Myself, and I. You are not available to love him if your own needs are more important to you than his.

Selfishness and self-love are not the same. Selfishness is willing to pay Saks Fifth Avenue prices for its own happiness and bargain basement prices for another's. Self-love says "I'm worth it, but so are you. Getting mine won't stop me from contributing to yours."

**Say it:** "When my eyes are so fixed on myself, I am blind to the light of my mate's love and I miss the privilege of embracing it. I choose a love that offers much to you, rather than only demands much from you."

**Do it:** Take one minute to describe in detail the most selfish person you know. Use lots of adjectives. Be specific and explicit. In what ways are you similar? Admit it. What would you like to see change about that? Commit to immediately begin making those changes.

# *13.* ▲ *Never Be Too Easy to Get*

*"Saturday morning I was at the mall early shopping for bras and panties, of all things. Just as I was leaving Victoria's Secret up walks this man with the most gorgeous eyes I have ever seen. I looked at him and he looked at me and said, 'Hi.' I guess he's kind of shy, because he kept on walking toward Sears. I caught up with him. We talked for a few minutes and I thought he was so nice; and I found out he was unattached. Well after we talked awhile and he didn't get around to asking, I made sure to give him my phone number. I gave him home, work, my pager, and my neighbor's number, just in case. As he turned to go, he said maybe he'd call me sometime. I told him to feel free to call this evening, and I asked him what time I should expect to hear from him. I wanted to be sure to be home. He didn't give a specific time, so I told him I would just go home and stay in today until I heard from him. I really didn't mind at all. He laughed, like he thought I was kidding. A few minutes after we went our separate ways, a great idea hit me. I ran all through Sears looking for him until I found him in the bedding department. I invited him to come over for dinner that night. That way I knew I'd get a chance to see him again. He promised he'd get back to me later to talk about it. I went home and stayed there all day waiting for his call. I never heard from him. I imagine he lost my numbers somewhere in the mall."*

*—Nona*

Men absolutely love the thrill of a chase. What takes some effort for him means far more to him than what doesn't. He's at his best when he must call upon his wit, savvy, and ingenuity to catch your eye and capture your heart.

Don't play standoffish, hard to get, or above it all; but *never* be too anxious, available, or accessible either. Men smell it. Show them your interest and your enthusiasm, just don't show it all at once. Give it to him piece by piece.

If you're one of those women who stumble all over themselves trying to get noticed by him ("Pick me! Pick me! Please pick me!"), rest assured they notice you all right, *and* they talk about you when you're not around. Believe me, you'd hate to hear what they say.

Maintain some mystique, but not aloofness. Avoid anything that looks like either desperation or lack of interest. Either extreme will only keep you out of the action. Make yourself abundantly pursuable.

- Be happy to see him—but not miserable if you don't.
- Gladly pick up the phone—but not on the first ring.
- Say yes to his invitations—but not all of them.
- Enjoy good times together—but don't volunteer to plan them all.
- Speak freely—but don't share every thought in your head.

Let him seek, *then* let him find. Let him knock, *then* open the door. Let him ask, *then* answer the request. If in any of these you reverse the order, you are way too easy to get.

**Say it:** "I am a prize worthy of his pursuit."

**Do it:** Call on your most caring friend and harshest critic. Ask her evaluation of where you fall on the scale between too easy to get (desperate) and too hard to know (uninterested). What changes in your style would bring balance?

# 14. ■ ◆ ◗
## *Let Your Guard Down*
## *(But Don't Forget How to Use It)*

*"I've gotten so used to being all business—no fun and games—at the office that I probably go too far with it when I leave work. Just the other day, this brother who lives in my building saw me at the swimming pool and stopped to talk, very polite and cordial—the whole nine yards . . . But when he asked for my phone number, there I was, all stiff and pulled back. He probably thought I was about to have him make his request in writing. I don't know, for some reason even when I'm interested, I can be a very hard person to get to know."*

*—Renee*

You, and everyone else who has ever pursued satisfying love relationships, have taken some hard knocks and crushing blows somewhere along the way. Rejection, unreciprocated love, and failed expectations have made the road to flourishing relationships rocky at best.

Nobody likes a punch in the nose, a slap in the face, or an assault on their self-esteem, and when we get one we instinctively know to put our guard up the next time. Only, since we don't know when the next time might be, some of us choose to keep our guard up all the time. If you're emotionally guarded all the time you probably feel a whole lot safer—and a whole lot lonelier too.

Pursuing love, and being in love, puts you in quite a vulnerable position. Your vulnerability is very appealing to the man who wants to love you with sensitivity and tenderness. Unfortunately it's also appealing to the one who takes pleasure in overpowering the vulnerable.

Intimate and long-lasting relationships cannot happen if there are massive stone walls around you and you're only seen and known through a few tiny peepholes. Even if you feel it was wisdom that guided you there, at some point courage must guide you out.

Let some Black man who seems deserving get close enough to touch and hold you. No, there are no up-front guarantees—"seems deserving" is as good as it gets. Consider letting your guard down by:

- Stopping to converse, instead of running off so fast (always so busy!).
- Abandoning yourself to fun with him that threatens to mess up your hair, break a nail, or dirty your jeans.
- Saying yes to seeing him during the time of the month when you feel least attractive.
- Reaching out to hold his hand, even if he hasn't done it first.
- Going ahead and telling him about the thing that you find most delightful in all the world.

Letting down your guard will mean gaining confidence in your own intuition—that inner voice that tells you "go ahead, it's okay" or "slow down, danger ahead."

Remember, the Black man in front of you has as much to lose as you do. He's vulnerable too.

**Say it:** "The things I do to protect myself from hurt have the side effects of making my world too small, tight, and lonely. In spite of the tension between wisdom and courage, I'll breathe deeply and begin to drop my guard."

**Do it:** What's the name of the man in your world who deserves even a bit more of you than you've been willing to give? If you lowered your guard, even a little, what do you envision saying or doing the next time you see him? Why not do it and say it the next time you see him?

# 15. ■❯ *Trust Him Until You Have Good Reason Not To*

*"Men usually think that I'm the most generous woman they've ever seen. I'm more than willing to give. It really doesn't matter to me: If I love you and I have it— whatever it is—you've got it. Actually that's only true about me when it comes to externals, not my insides. What most guys soon notice is that I don't trust very easily or very quickly. They can have what I've got, but not who I am. I know I hold back, even far into the relationship. It's hard for me to let them know my feelings all the time, because I'm not sure what they will do with them. It's like I wait for a signed guarantee that he can be trusted to handle me right. You can end up waiting forever to get that. I do not trust easily. I just don't."*

*—Xenia*

Black men crave the trust of the women who love them. When you trust him you show him you believe he measures up to all that is good, right, and honorable. More importantly, your trust assures him that you believe he is trying hard. Trusting him is a way of showing you approve of him. Your approval is pure gold to the man in your life.

The more he feels trusted by you the more trustworthy he is likely to become. Since he views your trust as something to be earned by his performance, integrity has great personal reward for him.

Don't start out with the assumption he cannot be trusted, and that he must prove otherwise to you before he can gain your confidence in him. That's finding him guilty until proven innocent—an unfair burden of proof.

Start out with confidence in him and give him every opportunity to sustain your confidence by his consistency. That's finding him innocent until proven guilty.

His trustworthiness should be evidenced by his commitment to make a few promises and keeping the ones he makes, by handling your love with sensitivity and respect, and by being consistent and honest. Significant or repeated violations of any of these are good reasons to consider repossessing your trust.

**Say it:** "He can appreciate my trust, and I can appreciate his trustworthiness. Trusting him until I have reason not to is not so much a gamble as it is an investment in a future with the kind of trust he desires and the trustworthiness I require."

**Do it:** Evaluate a past or present relationship with a Black man. How well did you/do you communicate that you trust him? What could you have done, or could you do, differently to make your confidence in his trustworthiness more clearly communicated? When will you start?

# 16. ▲ ■ ◆ Give Him, and Yourself, Permission to Fail

*"I think it's especially hard for people like Carl and me who've both already experienced one failed marriage apiece. We want this one to work so much that we can go overboard trying to be perfect spouses. Both of us try pretty hard to be what the other needs and, of course, we don't want to be guilty of the same mistakes we made in our previous marriages. We've finally figured out that anybody who lives with you 24/7 for the rest of your days is going to let you down sometimes—and you're going to let them down. We've decided we've got to relax around our failures. It's funny, when we got married we wrote our own vows. One part of it said, 'I will love, honor, and cherish you in spite of the mutual*

*disappointments of our inevitable failures ...' It sounded like just beautiful words at the time. Now it really means something to us, because we have to live it."*

—*Fayette*

When a man and a woman commit to loving each other, all kinds of strange and wonderful things can and do happen. Failure is one of them. True love never fails, but lovers do, and often miserably. Your relationship with a Black man has to be a place where some failure—yours and his—is expected, allowed, and even welcomed.

Sure, you do well to strive for excellence in love, tending well to each other's feelings, needs, expectations, hopes, and fears. You truly want to succeed at investing your selves in the cherishing of another with your whole heart, soul, mind, and strength. You want to ... You try to ... You mean to ... and from time to time you fail too.

We try to always think, say, feel, and do the right thing by each other, observing all the rules and regulations of romance—the do's and don'ts, shoulds and shouldn'ts. And if we try hard to abide by the rules ourselves, you'd better believe we try even harder to enforce them on our mates.

It's easy to become so focused on the "He done me wrong/I done him right" laws, and end up missing out on true intimacy. You can become so obsessed with doing it right that perfection becomes your lover and your man is just somebody you have on the side. You can't do it all right, all of the time. Sometimes, lovers flunk in the school of love.

Perfection, although worthy as a goal, is worthless as a requirement. Love offers another person a permit to fumble and even to fall. But often the fall is in a forward direction, and when the fallen one rises and regroups he is closer to the goal than before he fell.

Fatal failure is the failure to try, the failure to take risks and expand the limits of your love. It's safe and it's easy ... and it's a bore. Fulfilling failure is trying together, often succeeding, sometimes failing, and trying some more. It's risky—and exciting. Keep the focus on sharing the effort together, not being obsessed with the results.

**Say it:** "Like it says in the Bible, 'Love is patient and kind. Love does not remember wrongs done against it. Love trusts, hopes, and continues.' "

**Do it:** List five separate times in your life when you believed yourself to have failed. Can you see some good in those failures now that you didn't see then? Name each failure and say aloud, "It was also a success because _____."

# 17. ■◆ *Master the Art of Giving and Receiving Apologies*

*"Of course I could have simply said something like 'I'm sorry, I was wrong ...' and gone on about my business. Because I really was sorry and wished I hadn't handled the situation the way I did. But for some reason I feel so stupid saying something like that. I swear, I did everything on earth to show him I was sorry but I couldn't bring myself to say the words. I organized his sock drawer, picked up his dry cleaning, and was on my way to get his car washed. That's when Roderick said: 'Uh, Miss Lady, wouldn't it be easier to just say "I'm sorry?" ' "*

*—Cynthia*

Nobody likes to say "I'm sorry." Even when we do it, it's more often because we feel we should, and not because we want to. Saying "I'm sorry" is the same as saying "I was wrong." Confessing we were wrong is a dreadful assault on our pride. And whether you like it or not, loving someone constantly positions us for assaults on our pride.

Receiving apologies isn't any less challenging. When your man says "I'm sorry" it is hard to know just what response to offer back. On the one hand, you want to be gracious enough to accept his apology and forgive, while on the other hand you may not want his transgression to be so swiftly and easily pardoned. "I accept your apology" is easy to say. Yet it's hard to mean it when you're not sure if he meant it when he said "I'm sorry."

For Black men the apology issue is major. Both giving and receiving them requires large doses of humility. Men struggle with the fearful possibility that should he humble himself he will in some way be less in your eyes. Deep within, that thought scares him to death.

A secret for success in giving apologies to a Black man is to be action-oriented, not just feeling-oriented. Let him know what you are sorry about, but also what you plan to do about it in the future. For example: "I'm really sorry I scheduled my business trip on your birthday. From now on I'll coordinate with you before I finalize my travel plans."

The same principle works in the art of accepting his apology. Commitments to action are key. They provide substance and focus to words and emotions for a man. So when he sincerely apologizes to you, tell him, "I accept your apology for raising your voice at me, and [not *but*] I'd like to talk about what we can do to avoid that situation in the future."

The old song should perhaps more rightly declare, "Making up is hard to do." Falling out with each other and walking out on each other are pieces of cake compared to mastering the intricate patterns and shifting rhythms of the "I'm sorry" tango. Sometimes you will lead, and other times follow. You need to master both, or the party is over.

**Say it:** "How I handle giving and receiving apologies can be a bridge that brings us back to each other, or pushes us apart. For my part, I will offer and accept these two simple words: 'I'm sorry.'"

**Do it:** Begin to practice the use of action-oriented apologies as described above. Use it with whomever you owe an apology, or from whomever you receive one.

# 18. ▲ ■ ● ◆ ◗
## *Finish All Mess,*
## *Then Let It Stay Finished*

*"Usually when we're having some major drama between us—an argument, or a big fuss-fight, I am so stunned and angry I just want to get out for a minute. I keep feeling like I need to go and collect my thoughts and my words, then come back and resolve the matter with him. Instead, I have a habit of making him think we've settled the matter and I'm okay with it. But a lot of times I'm not okay with it at all. For the sake of peace and quiet, I give plenty of 'okay's and 'Yes, that's fine's that I don't really mean. Then, later, when I'm alone I'll replay the whole thing in my head: What he said, what I coulda/shoulda/woulda said, and by then I'm three hours, or three days more pissed off than when we argued. That's when I usually pick up the phone to really let him have it. When I do, he always responds with his same tired line, in his same annoyed, impatient tone, 'Monique, I thought we had settled this . . .'"*

*—Monique*

Let's be real about it: Somewhere in the midst of all your love and romance, cleaving and caressing, will come the sudden entrance of some form of mess. It's a fact of life. I know it, and so do you. There are, of course, several varieties of mess, each more aggravating and frustrating than the other:

- Misunderstanding ("That's not what I meant and you know it . . . !") mess.
- Insecurity ("So what's the matter, I'm not _____ [you fill in the blank]") mess.

- Jealousy ("Why don't you just pack your stuff and go on over to her place!") mess.
- Angry ("Who in the world do you think you are . . . !") mess.
- Vengeful ("I'll get you, if it's the last thing I do . . . !") mess.

The list is never-ending. Mess happens, and sooner or later it will happen to you and the Black man you love.

In your relationship you may experience more or less mess than others you know. Yours may be mostly "firecracker mess" (it's quick, it's loud, and it's over), or maybe "bonfire mess" (it's big, it's hot, and you keep throwing more junk on it).

Whatever kind of mess may occur, it can and often does violently derail the relationship. Mess happens. What you do when it does makes all the difference in the world.

The two most common mess-management mistakes are:

MISTAKE No. 1: Never getting around to finishing it: Unfinished mess doesn't politely excuse itself, never to return again. It hangs in the air, taking up space as it grows, and tries to suffocate the life right out of your love for each other. Talk it out, fight it out, but come hell or high water—finish all mess. Don't rest until mess has been processed, recycled, and transformed into something useful. Mess that you don't finish becomes mess that finishes you.

MISTAKE No. 2: Resurrecting old, dead mess: There is little more damaging than resurrecting old mess and piling it on top of the new. Don't give in to the temptation to rerun mess from bygone days, in the heat of handling fresh, new mess. It's unfair, and it announces to your mate that "all weapons are legal!" Fight the urge to fight unfairly. Let settled mess stay buried.

**Say it:** "Ignoring mess is not a healthy option, neither is burying it only to resurrect it later. As much as it is within my power, I will rush to resolve and refrain from reviving our mess."

**Do it:** Sit down with your mate and establish some policies and procedures for mess management (conflict resolution) in your relationship. Decide together what's fair and what's not. Above all, agree never to replay old mess. (Warning: Don't wait until there's a big mess between you before you do this. You'll find it's way too late.)

# *19.* ■ ◆ *Avoid the Sapphire Syndrome*

*"My license plate frame, my coffee mug, and my favorite sweatshirt all say 49% SWEETHEART, 51% BITCH. I get tickled whenever I look at them. But when Marvin says, 'You know you're acting like a real . . .' I swear, he'd better act as if there is no letter B in the alphabet!"*

*—Carole*

"Sapphire." She's an unfortunate and much-despised stereotype—a swivel-necked, hip-holding, eye-rolling, teeth-sucking, acid-tongued caricature of the women who love Black men.

You could be suffering from Sapphire Syndrome if:

- You cut him off or often demand he "hurry up" when he is speaking to you.
- You have little to say to him when you're satisfied, but much to say when you're angry.
- You tell him to shut up, and he does—permanently.
- You frequently call him by name—but seldom his own.
- Your conversations with him have few of these: ???, and lots of these: !!!.
- You use high-volume threats and ultimatums to motivate, persuade, or "instruct" him.
- You experience a secret glow of satisfaction when he looks more like a hurt little boy than a self-assured man.
- You can't help making demeaning references to his sexual organs and abilities—even when the conversation isn't about sex.

- You boast to your friends about how you "set him straight," "fixed his butt," or "busted his bubble," and you encourage them to do the same thing with their men.
- Nothing makes you angrier or gets more protest from you than when he dares call you a "Sapphire."

Insecurity and self-centeredness flow in the veins of those who suffer from the Sapphire Syndrome. They are both toxic. They cripple, paralyze, and ultimately render love comatose.

Recovery from the Sapphire Syndrome involves admitting to the diagnosis and consistently doing the opposite of what Sapphire would do. Where she would normally go into overdrive, becoming overbearing and assaultive, downshift to a calm, steady demeanor. Where she might normally assume a detached "I don't give a damn" posture, show a more open, receptive attitude.

**Say it:** "I know I have a natural love for Black men. But I sometimes seem to have an evil twin sister named Sapphire who lives in me and is gratified by deflating Black manhood. I must increase, she must decrease. Better yet, she has got to go."

**Do it:** Imagine Oprah doing a show on "Women with Sapphire Syndrome." Would you be a subject, the expert, or an audience member? Which one? Why? What would you say?

# 20. ■ ◆ *Let Some Battles Pass*

*"Ray and I never have been the type to cuss and scream and throw things across the room at each other. We've had our disagreements and ticked each other off sometimes, but I guess we've finally learned what's worth fighting about and what's not. It's not that either one of us is the quiet, mousy type. We know how to get it on,*

*head-to-head and toe-to-toe, and wear each other out. I think, though, we both know that the other isn't going anywhere, and every dispute doesn't have to be fought out, every time. Some of them we just let slide. I can guarantee you that when there is something that we need to get ugly about we haven't forgotten how to do that either."*

*—Lydia*

This may come as a complete shock to you but, contrary to popular opinion, some fights just don't have to be fought. Some differences just don't merit discussion or dialogue or a full-force, in-your-face argument. There are certainly more than enough conflicts in any significant relationship to claim your undivided attention. But some of them aren't worth the breath it takes to say, "Hold on a minute, we are going to deal with this right now." Let some battles pass.

Perhaps this strikes you as an outrageous concept in an age when women who love Black men are constantly encouraged to be more assertive, to speak their minds, and to "take no crap." The truth of the matter is, there are certain kinds of conflict issues that when battled over only deplete your time and energy and settle little or nothing. Sure, the two of you get a chance to sharpen your fighting skills, but for those unworthy problems that's about all you get. Ignore them.

The types of battles you should let pass are the kind that weaken your relationship rather than strengthen it, that tear down rather than build. They provide lots of fireworks, but no heat and no lasting light.

- If fighting the battle only establishes who's the winner and who's the loser, let it pass.
- If fighting the battle is not for the sake of getting rid of an intimacy obstacle, but just a pet peeve, let it pass.
- If fighting the battle is simply your opportunity to let off some steam that's really owed to someone else, let it pass.
- If fighting the battle is merely to enforce your compulsive, perfectionistic, nitpicky standards, let it pass.
- If fighting the battle would be for the sake of childish ego-stroking—yours or his—let it pass.

Use the precious time and energy you have conserved to invest in resolving conflicts that matter, and will matter far into the future.

**Say it:** "There are some battlefields that you'll never catch me on. It is neither surrender nor retreat, it is me being wise about what wars are worth it, and which ones aren't."

**Do it:** During the next seven days identify one potential battle to let pass in your interaction with a Black man. After you do it, reflect on how you felt stronger and more powerful for having done so.

# 21. Celebrate His Victories, Celebrate His Efforts

*"It was such a tense time for him leading up to taking the bar exam. He worked all week, studied every night, and then was in the library all weekend. We hardly ever saw each other. I knew he felt kind of guilty because he kept apologizing about it. He had warned that it was going to be rough for a while, but I don't think either of us expected it to be that consuming. By the time he went to take the exam he was a nervous wreck. So much was riding on how well he would do—years of school, his career plans, everything. After it was all over he came by. When he walked in he saw the champagne, and the little congratulations cake I had picked up. He was so surprised. He said, 'Isn't this a little bit premature? We won't know the results for a couple of months.' I rushed to correct him: 'Oh no baby, we're not celebrating the results tonight. We're celebrating how hard you tried—no matter what the results are.' He loved that."*

*—Brenda*

People who succeed at everything they attempt need no support or encouragement from anyone. Perfection carries its own rewards. Mere mortals, like the man in your life, however, are at their best when they are sure that the women who love them will celebrate their efforts, as well as their victories.

Performance and accomplishment are major themes for Black men. For him, winning means doing it right and making it happen. It's the warrior/conqueror spirit in him. That means his life is a series of attempts at winning and succeeding (or even a good attempt to make an attempt). Sometimes his efforts lead to success, and sometimes they don't. Nothing matters more than your commitment to heartily commend him for both.

The marathon runner who didn't come in first, the candidate who lost by a few votes, and the Academy Award nominee who goes home empty-handed all have this in common: They tried really hard, and the rest of us honor their efforts.

Literally or figuratively, throwing a party for sincere effort alone is quite in order. Well-celebrated efforts often lead to full-out success stories.

Don't let him, or yourself, get away with not recognizing efforts as well as achievements in his career, his personal goals, or in your relationship with each other. He tries, and trying has to count for something.

Stop along the path of progress and make mention of how far he's come in what he's attempting. Tell him and show him that both victory, and the efforts to achieve it, are highly esteemed in your eyes. And, as far as you are concerned, they are always cause for cork-popping, band-playing, noise-making, confetti-throwing celebrations.

**Say it:** "It is my privilege and my pleasure to be his one-woman celebration committee. I am committed to this Black man never being without a cheerleader."

**Do it:** Make your own survey. For the next week simply ask at least one Black man daily (including your mate), "What really makes you feel your efforts and successes are celebrated?" Use what you learn to celebrate your man's efforts and successes.

# 22. ▲ ■ ● ◆ ◗
## Point Out His Power

*"Sometimes I think my husband, Earnest, is so busy trying to become better and better at everything he does that he doesn't even notice how well he's already doing. For instance, I have never seen a man who takes being a good father so seriously. He loves our children so much, and he gives them the kind of attention they need. He's great, and the kids worship him, but Earnest is always second-guessing himself about parenting. He wonders if he did or said the right thing all the time. He's got fathering, and a bunch of other things, down so well and everybody knows it but him."*

*—Mary Alice*

There are lots of ways to analyze and explain how Black men can walk around feeling insignificant. The theorizing usually includes talk of slavery, discrimination, socioeconomic struggle, and negative stereotyping. You've heard them all, and he has probably felt the effects of them all. Inside the man you love, and in his brothers far and wide, are three very private and persistent questions that demand answers: Do I have any power in this world? Do I have any control over anything? And if I don't, how much worth could I possibly have?

For men, power means having what it takes to accomplish the tasks that go along with being a man. His chief concern in life is "Will I be able to pull it off?" Whatever the "it" may be. Be assured this kind of power doesn't mean domination over you, or anybody else, nor is it about sovereign rule over the universe. It's about being capable and confident. Black men yearn for that. And more than anyone, the women who love them can help them get it.

You can't bestow a sense of power upon him or produce it for him, but you can point it out to him. You do that when you reassure him that he is capable, valuable, and even impressive. He has a secret hunger for your reassurance.

Men are taught, and have learned all too well, that they shouldn't need anything from anybody. For them masculinity is measured by the degree of self-sufficiency he has or hasn't got. That's why you will seldom, if ever, hear him ask for the reassuring reminders that he treasures so highly.

Work to boost the ego of the man you love. He is probably not as self-confident as he appears. He is especially helped by the things you say that communicate that you find him to be "man enough" in the areas of his life where he has the most self-doubt.

In what areas does he show himself to be a strong and able man? His leadership style? His fathering? His skill and sensitivity at lovemaking? His clear thinking in a crisis? His compassion, integrity, or patience? Whatever they are, tell him what you see. Especially in the areas where he strives with diligence, yet struggles with self-confidence.

**Say it:** "I will be his power-pack. I will help him see what I see that is powerfully positive and positively powerful in him."

**Do it:** Get together with your man solely to point out each other's positive attributes, abilities, and actions. Acknowledge to him, in detail, how capable, how powerful and impressive he is. Today and every tomorrow that you have applaud him. (Note: Standing ovations work best.)

# 23. ▲ ■ ● ◆ ◗ Reality-Check Your Expectations of Him

*"Sometimes it's hard for me to commit myself to any one option because I'm afraid I'll miss out on a better one later. It makes settling on an apartment or a car, or even a new hairstyle, difficult. It's an even bigger problem when I do that*

*with men. The minute I get a little rhythm from a man I start measuring all of his qualifications to see if he matches my idea of Mr. Perfect. That's how I almost missed out on Ben. I always expected that anyone I got serious with would be an upwardly mobile professional, or I couldn't be happy with him. Ben is a short, average-looking city bus driver—and he is wonderful to me. I am so glad he stuck around long enough for me to learn that tall, dark, and handsome with a briefcase is not the only form wonderful guys come in."*

*—Syntelle*

The hardest part of living real life is accepting the realities we find there. Fantasy is so much more exhilarating. Wouldn't it be wonderful if everything about your relationship operated according to your own personally designed fantasy? Then, whatever you expect would be what you get. You, and you alone, would creatively whip up the version of reality that pleases you most. Best of all, no matter what you expect of the Black man you love, it would be perfectly and completely in sync with reality. Your reality . . . Wouldn't it be wonderful?

All right, all right—snap out of it. It's time to wake up now. Like it or not, there is but one reality to return to. It's a place where people, places, and things are the way they are—not necessarily the way you would like them to be.

In real-life relationships, the woman who loves a Black man does well to reality-check her own perceptions and expectations of him from time to time. She must unflinchingly ask and answer the questions: Is what I am expecting of this man at this moment reality-based? Is it mostly fact, or mostly fiction? Is it fair to him for me to hold this expectation of him? Honest answers and necessary adjustments can save you and him some major grief.

The more that what you expect of how he looks, thinks, behaves, relates, communicates, and operates is based on realistic notions of who men are in general, and who he is in particular, the more you can avoid frustration and disappointment. Both of which can sabotage what may be, realistically speaking, a good relationship with one who is, in reality, a pretty decent Black man.

Expectations of him that test too high ("my knight in shining armor") on the fantasy/reality scale set him up for failure and you for resentment. Expectations that test too low ("my low-down loser of a man") present no challenge to his negative traits and set you up for resentment again.

When you begin to experience the joys of a profound love, it is not unusual to expect the one you love to have an almost magical effect on your life—wiping away all sorrows, healing all hurts, filling all empty places, and generally making all things new. That's far too much to expect from love, or from any lover. Check in with reality, simplify your expectations, and learn to let good enough be good enough. Get real.

**Say it:** "I acknowledge that real life is seldom as warm and inviting as fantasy. But there is too much in real life to miss out on by waiting around for fantasies to become reality. I will check myself, before I wreck myself."

**Do it:** On one sheet of paper, write a thorough description of your expectations of the man you love (or hope one day to love). Include expectations of his looks, personality, behavior, character traits, abilities and resources, and so forth. Turn to the front of the book and compare your description to the Raw Deal, Ideal, and Real Deal Black man on pages 8–10. Which does your description come closest to? Why? Now on that same sheet of paper complete this sentence honestly and concretely: "To make my image of Black men more balanced and more realistic I need to remember . . ." (Be very specific.)

# 24. ▲ ■ ● ◆ ◗
## *Find Something About Him to Believe in Every Day*

*"He's always been an early riser and I'm a night owl. It's not at all uncommon for me to be moving around the house, doing who knows what, long after he's gone to bed and is sound asleep. When I finally come to our bedroom, a lot of times I will stop, without even planning to, and just look at him lying there. I hear his faint snore and for a brief moment, or sometimes several, I study that perfectly*

*peaceful look on his face. It's dark and the room is very still. I linger over him awhile and usually begin to think about just how good a man he really is. It starts slowly, like a short list, until my mind becomes flooded with different things I respect and appreciate about him. There is so much. It's in those few seconds in the dark with him fast asleep that I remember just how taken I am with him."*

*—Maxine*

The truth is you really don't have to love Black men in general, or any one of them in particular. If you love one it's because you can and you choose to, not because you must. Your love and your efforts to show it only make sense because somewhere on the inside you hold the belief that he is worth it. In order for love to grow, that belief must be nurtured on a daily basis.

Just as deep-rooted and strong-limbed oak trees can nearly reach heaven when given rich soil, regular rain, and warming sun, a Black man grows and flourishes in the knowledge of your faith and confidence in him. It makes all the difference in the world to him that you keep on keeping on, because you believe in him.

Negative propaganda about Black men is served up daily, in generous portions, by many, from wounded and weary sisters to the narrow and incriminating images on the six o'clock news. All of it can gradually erode your faith in him. You can't afford to let it.

Loving him, and seeing that love grow rather than diminish, requires a daily search for the many reasons you had to love him in the first place. If you keep your eyes firmly fixed there, you will discover that previously unknown and highly endearing traits in your man will keep springing into your view.

Every day find one more "something about him" to cast your confidence upon. Some days, it will be right in front of your face, no less visible than the multifaceted brilliance of a near-flawless diamond. On other days, you will need to seek it out with a magnifying glass, a fine-tooth comb, and a forgiving sense of humor.

No need trying to see something wonderful in him that's not really there. Rather, make a daily search-and-seizure expedition into the remotest parts of his interior, through his mud-filled swamps, his grassy meadowlands, and his craggy mountain ranges. Each day, don't rest until you grab hold of something worth believing in about him. Small or great, subtle or dramatic, for his sake and yours, seek and you will find.

**Say it:** "My love for him is in direct proportion to my belief in him as a man who is worth it. Honestly, gladly, tenaciously, I will search daily for one more reason to be confident that my love is well placed in him."

**Do it:** On the first of next month start to write on the calendar each day one concrete reason why you love him and have confidence in him. Let each day be different, no repeats. At the end of the month write him an intimate love letter, and attach the calendar page.

# 25. ▲ ■ ● ◆ ◗
## *Treasure Some Things Simply Because You Know He Does*

*"Donald loves reggae music. He's got every Bob Marley–looking, ganga-smoking, dreadlock-wearing, Rasta man album that ever came out. You'd think Donald was born in Montego Bay instead of straight out of Houston. Frankly, I can't stand reggae. It gives me a headache after five minutes. Sometimes I tease him, telling him, if I come over and hear reggae playing, I won't even knock—I'll just turn around and go home and put on some real music. He pays that absolutely no attention, because he knows how many Saturday mornings I'm down at different music stores, rummaging through the reggae section to find something that Donald doesn't have. You know I always walk out of those stores happily carrying another CD for Donald as if it were made of gold. I enjoy doing that because I know how much it means to him."*

*—Nicole*

One of the most loving things one human being can do for another is to place a high value on something simply because someone you love does. It says, "I treasure the people, places, or things that are special to you, because they are special to you." What you are really saying is, "You are special to me."

For a man, what he thinks about and what he enjoys are treasures in his private world. He does not see them as pieces and props separate from himself; they are critical components of his very identity and what make his life have meaning.

Maybe it's his friendships, his career, his favorite way of relaxing, the foods he loves, his home, car, clothes, his hobbies, or his God. You can tell they are his treasures when no matter what he consistently makes room for them in his life and they consistently switch on his "Pleased, Satisfied, and Content" button.

To you, it may be "just stuff," but it's stuff he adores, and it occupies the top shelves of his internal trophy case.

Your love for him shines brilliantly when he knows you treasure what he treasures, simply because he does, and not because it holds the same meaning or has the same appeal in your private world. Maybe what he treasures is not your kind of person, place, or thing at all, but you are turned on by seeing him turned on.

**Say it:** "I will keep my eyes open to see what things put a spark in my man's eyes. When I see it I will rush to stand with him in the glow that spark ignites. I will treasure what he treasures, for love's sake."

**Do it:** Whether it's a first date or fiftieth, or after years of marriage, interview your man. Ask him what are the twenty most treasured people, places, or things in his world. Listen and learn what parts of him are connected to those treasures.

# 26. ▲ ● *Let Him Ask for What He Wants (Don't Assume)*

*"When Patrick mentioned that he wanted to go all out celebrating his thirty-fifth birthday, I geared up to make it happen beyond anything he could have expected. I assumed that celebrating meant a big party with lots of people and the works. And of course I figured . . . Okay, I assumed, again, that a surprise party would make it an even 'mo better' celebration. I set it all up, invited all his friends and family, people from his job, his workout partners, and—check this out—even his old girlfriend. I assumed he'd love the surprise, have a ball, and appreciate my thoughtfulness and creativity forever. I was wrong. That's how I found out there's nothing he hates more than surprises. Patrick said I was wrong to assume so much having asked him so little."*

*—Adelle*

Guessing what a Black man really wants from you, and trying to give it to him before he asks, only works if you are trying to give yourself a migraine headache. A good habit to break—or to avoid from the jump—is assuming you already know exactly what he wants and that you're responsible for getting it to him.

Maybe you are a strong believer in the "if you really love somebody, you should know what they want before they ask" principle. But if you really love someone, and want to give them what they really want—the *only* way to do that is to ask them.

Assuming what he wants leads to attempting to make, give, do, or be it. That leads only to anger if you are wrong or if he doesn't show enough appreciation for your efforts. Your actions, based on assumptions, instead of his requests, are like a sweaty tap dance you do to music only he can hear, and getting no applause because you were out of step in the first place!

When a woman assumes and acts upon the assumption, her man will accept and appreciate it—as long as her assumption is accurate. When it's not, he becomes annoyed and aggravated because he feels unheard and disregarded. "Why," he wonders, "didn't she give me a chance to speak for myself?"

At the root of this guessing and giving game is an all too urgent need to please. Check yourself; if you find yourself working to give him that for which he has not asked, then remember: Whether he wants your help, your advice, sex, or even your hand in marriage, let him *ask* for it.

**Say it:** "Mind-reading is not now, nor will it ever be, a talent I possess. I give up trying. When I A-S-S-U-M-E, I make an ASS of U and of ME."

**Do it:** Think before you go out of your way for him: "What am I about to do, and why exactly am I about to do it?" If it's mostly for your sake, or something you *think* (but don't know) is for him, reconsider. If it's mostly for his sake, ask him and then do it, if you're willing and able.

# 27. ▲ ■ ● ◆ ◗ Give Him Time to Process His Emotions and to Understand Yours

*"I get so frustrated with Daryl when I want to know how he's feeling about something and all I get from him is 'Okay.' I can usually see on his face, or tell by his tone of voice, that he is feeling something. But by the way he reacts you would think I had asked him to explain nuclear physics or something. What makes it*

*worse is when he later tells me I'm not considering his feelings in a decision. How can I consider them, when I don't even know what his feelings are?"*

—*Celia*

One of the greatest gifts you will ever give the Black man you love is time. He needs loads of it—far more than you do—to figure out his own feelings, and certainly to understand yours. The more intense the feelings the more time it will take him to know them and to share them. Men are much more at home in the outer world. They are quick to grasp the tangible, material, and the concrete. When it comes to emotions (intangible, nonmaterial, and nonconcrete) they feel the feelings, but they can feel them a long time before they know what feelings they are. He can't share with you what he hasn't accessed himself. That's where your patience comes in. He needs it desperately—and if you're the woman who loves him, he needs it from you.

As a woman, you are likely to have much more rapid access to your feelings. One minute you'll feel joy, or sadness, or embarrassment or rage, and in a matter of milliseconds you've already understood the source of your feelings and have begun to communicate them to your lover. He can do it too, but it may take him hours or even days. So let it.

Getting in touch with intense feelings and why they are present can be hard work. Women tend to do that work by relating, sharing, speaking, and exploring together. Men are the opposite. They tend to do their emotional work in the privacy of their own brooding thoughts and extended silences. They kick back, zone out, shut down, or otherwise go "underground" to get a handle on what they feel and why they feel it. Only then is he willing and able to share those feelings with you.

For his sake and yours, let him go underground. Don't pressure him to share his feelings with you ("Talk to me. Tell me what you're feeling, *now!*") until he's returned and is ready to report his findings. Otherwise, he'll be sure to make a mess of it. He'll use lots of words to provide you an answer. But if he hasn't had time to process, he won't be telling you the truth. He won't even know what the truth is yet!

When you and your man are experiencing some intensely emotional times— commitment-making, dispute-settling, face-saving, forgiveness-seeking—communicating your feelings and understanding each other is crucial. At those times, simply preface your request with these three words, "When you can . . . ," as in "When you can, will you tell me how you are feeling about this?" Or "When you can, will you tell me what you understand about my feelings on this." Or try the "chocolate, vanilla, or strawberry" approach: "When you can, would you tell me if it's anger, or fear, or frustration, or something else that you are feeling?"

"When you can . . ." frees him to take the time he needs to go underground, and it makes it clear that you are confident he will return better prepared to share emotional material with you. Can men share their emotions? Absolutely. Can the women who love them help them do it? Positively, with time.

**Say it:** "I will not fear the time or the method that my man uses to bring me his feelings or lay hold to mine. I release him to his underground and trust him to return more aware of my feelings and ready to offer me his own."

**Do it:** Get comfortable using "When you can . . ." Use it by looking him in his eyes, keeping a calm but determined tone, and if he procrastinates on a return to the issue repeat as often as needed, "When you can, I would appreciate it if . . ."

# 28. ▲ ■ ● ◆ ◗
## *Don't Make Him Guess What You Want*

*"I want Ronnie to do for me what I try to do for him. When he's around, I'm constantly looking out for what would make him happy, so I can do it for him. I've always believed that if you really love someone you should show that by trying to give them their heart's desire. When I was home with the flu last week, Ronnie came over to keep me company. But he really wasn't much help. He sat with me all day long, and if I wanted some juice or a magazine or my pillow fluffed—or anything—I had to ask, otherwise I'd still be waiting to get it."*

*—Corinn*

To men, your silence means one thing: that everything is just fine with you the way things are. To him, if you are not requesting, demanding, or protesting anything, nothing's broke; and if it ain't broke he won't try to fix it. The best thing you could do for him and for yourself is to ask for what you want. There's no guarantee that you'll always get it, but at least you give him something clear and concrete to either deliver or deny. He can use his energy to respond to your need, rather than to guess what it is.

A common false belief, held by many women who love Black men, is that real love means either: (a) He should already know what I want or need; or (b) If he doesn't know he should take it upon himself to ask, and ask, and ask . . . Men are much better at loving by giving and doing, than at asking and guessing. To get the best of his love, open your mouth and state your case.

Men love to satisfy their women's desires. It makes them feel quite capable and needed (both of which they love). But Black men despise hopping around to supply every selfish whim or wish-list item that their women make known. It makes them feel exploited. If you clearly communicate to him what you truly appreciate, believe me, he'll let you know one way or the other where he stands.

**Say it:** "I will never be without what I desire from the man I love because I did not make it known. He will know it because I will say it."

**Do it:** What do you want from him that you are not clearly making known to him? Before you ask him, ask yourself: Is this a realistic request? Is he the right person to ask it of? Is this the right time? If the answer is no to any one of these, table or trash your request. If the answer is yes, calmly, clearly, kindly ask for what you want.

# 29. ▲ ▶ *Don't Require That Your Every Need Be Met by Him*

*"I can be very outspoken, and I will stand up for myself when I know I'm right about something important. You should have seen me. I looked Gil dead in his eyes and told him, 'You are supposed to be my man, and yes, I do believe that means you should be there for me in any way that I need. What in the world do I need you for, if I am still going to be running around depending on other people for things, when we call ourselves a couple?'"*

—*Kamillah*

Even a perfect love relationship (if there is such a thing) won't meet every need of the individuals in it. Love is rich and full. But neither love nor your lover is ever enough to meet *all* your needs. Don't require it.

You are a complex human being, full of all kinds of nooks and crannies, underground passages and secret compartments. You have physical, psychological, spiritual and emotional needs, friendship needs, and recreational and intellectual needs, among others. Some of which the man in your life will supply, and some of which he won't. He can't. But don't worry. Love is still love even if some of your deepest needs are fulfilled outside it.

When you try to get every need, especially every emotional need, from one source—your lover—you'll end up with a lot of unfulfilled needs and he'll end up with a secret urge for a vacation—away from you.

The Black man in your life may try for a while to be your "Super-Incredible Needs-Meeter" (it flows naturally from his obsession with performance). It gives him a gratifying jolt of self-satisfaction to think *you* think he is all you'll ever need. Soon, though, both of you will find him lacking and both of you will end up very disappointed—with each other.

Don't make him your only source of life support. If you do, he's certain to go into overload and you'll go into a deep depression. Just like you did before you met the man you love, you should get different pieces of your needs met in different places. Remember "favorite" and "only" aren't synonymous.

- Maybe he's your favorite friend—don't require he be your only one.
- Maybe he's your favorite confidant and conversation sharer—don't require he be your only one.
- Maybe he's your favorite shopping mall partner or traveling companion—don't require he be your only one.
- Maybe he's your favorite comforter and advisor—don't require he be your only one.

Yours is a big life. Spread some of it around.

**Say it:** "I will love him with a love that refuses to cast him in the role of 'My One and Only' needs supplier. Relieving him of that burden makes it possible for him to be 'My First and Favorite.' "

**Do it:** Have a conversation with the man in your life about any of the ways that his responding to your needs has become burdensome or overwhelming to him and your relationship. Together, suggest some ways that you can shift some of your required needs to other appropriate relationships.

# 30. ▲ ■ ● ◆ ❱ Remind Him Often of Why You Choose to Love Him

*"He would probably think it was our honeymoon or an anniversary, or one of our romantic weekends away, something like that. But the moment that I remember feeling so much love for him that I almost couldn't stand it was last spring, around the end of April. The calendar told me that the summer swimsuit-wearing season was right around the corner. The mirror and the scale were telling me I was not ready. I made a vow to myself to do a few miles around the track in the park every morning to try to get myself together. On the first morning, I said goodbye to Bernard and set off. That first day was the hardest, and it was an unseasonably warm day to boot. I was really out of shape and I could feel it. After a few laps around the track I was drenched, and threatening to call it quits. Then, out of nowhere, Bernard appeared, walking right alongside me. From behind his back he presented me with an ice-cold bottle of Evian water. I was so surprised and so encouraged by that, I fell in love with that man all over again."*

*—Wendy*

God knows, you've got your reasons for loving the Black man in your life, but does that man know? I mean really know—not suspect, hope, or assume? At this very moment in time, does he know, beyond a shadow of doubt, how much you love him and why?

Whatever your feelings about him and commitment to him may be, you have made a choice to love him. It was no accident, no fluke of nature or mischief of the gods that you chose to love him, and daily you choose to continue. "Falling in love" makes the process sound so involuntary, so accidental, like "I fell into an open manhole." The phrase obscures the fact that love is a deliberate choice based on an assortment of "why"s and "wherefore"s. Regularly remind him (and yourself) what they are.

Why do you choose to love him? Is it his strong but gentle nurturing spirit? His wicked sense of humor and boisterous laugh? His one in a million outer packaging and his extraordinary sensuality? Is it his clever way with words and knowing use of silence? Or his iron-willed determination and infinite patience? Maybe it's the bowlike curve of his thighs, the fragrance at the center of his chest, or the him-and-him-alone way he says your name? Any of these? Maybe all of them and more. Remind him of them.

Never get so busy building a future together that you fail to revisit—together—the reasons that you loved him in the first place. Make a return trip there often. Simply say so. Out of nowhere, redeeming one of those unscheduled moments you have together, turn to him and say in your own way, "I choose to deeply love you today, because you _____" Or shout it from the rooftops. Write it in the sky. Declare it to the masses. But above all, Remind *him*.

**Say it:** "My love for him is not accidental. I love him on purpose and with good cause. Remembering why I do, and how much I do, helps remind us both that our worst of times are worth enduring, and our best of times are worth celebrating."

**Do it:** Carefully follow the following four steps with no substitutions or variations:

1. Remind your man of why you love him.
2. Remind him again.
3. Remind him once more.
4. Repeat steps 1 to 3.

# 31. ▲● *Commit to His Growth, Not Just His Comfort*

*"It was not my idea for us to go to Las Vegas in the first place. And it definitely wasn't my idea for Harvey to use his rent money to try and make a killing at the blackjack table. But it was his rent, and what he did with it was his business. I just warned him not to come running to me to bail him out if he lost it trying to get rich quick. He doubled his money within minutes—and, of course, within an hour he lost everything. His rent was gone. That's when he came right to me with the brilliant idea that I loan him the money. I have found, in situations like that, that the hardest word to pronounce is the word 'no.' But I said it, and I meant it too. It's tough, but I know I've got to let Harvey deal with the consequences of his own choices."*

*—Diane*

If you believe your highest priority should be making sure that the man you love stays comfortably unaffected by life's harsh realities, then you will do anything to keep him from feeling pain. You won't want him to suffer the painful consequences of his choices, or experience the demands of discipline, or the weighty encumbrances of responsibility. If you are committed to his comfort more than to his growth, you won't be able to stand it when his life is uncomfortable.

The process by which human beings grow wiser, more disciplined, responsible, and mature is struggle. Growth hurts.

If yours is a love that merely buffers, shields, or takes possession of his pain—

to keep him comfortable at all costs—your love is a fraud. You'll "love" him right out of the opportunity to grow up.

If yours is a love that is committed to his growth, you will say what needs to be said to him, when it needs to be said. You'll be dead-on-target honest, and sometimes it will be painful for him. Pain can strengthen us.

If you are committed to his growth, more than to his comfort, you will let him stand on his own two feet, even if his knees buckle from time to time. Standing *with* him will bless him. Standing *for* him will surely curse him.

Everyone who ever learned to live life richly, confidently, and triumphantly learned to endure the aches and pains that go with it—by having to. Isn't that how you got as sturdy and mature as you are? Don't rob the man in your life of his productive pain. If you can take it, you will be able to witness the residual traces of "boy" becoming "man" in the one you love.

Love him enough to be his travel companion on the road to personal growth and maturity, rather than his bodyguard within the walls of his comfort zone.

**Say it:** "His comfort is important to me. His growth is even more important. He, not I, must feel the consequences of his own choices. I will not run from the struggle of watching him struggle."

**Do it:** Look at your own life. Where have you seen necessary struggle produce growth of maturity and ability? Are you helping or hindering that same process in the man in your life? Make loving changes.

# 32. *Ask His Opinion, Value His Opinion*

*"I think the first phase of dating someone new is going through the 'I can top that' stage. That's when he'll comment about something—probably to show you how well-informed and insightful he is—and you'll say something even more clever to*

*show him you're no slouch either. Eventually you stop that foolishness and start listening to what each other has to say. That's when I found out just how interesting he can be. He usually has some unique point of view or thought-provoking tidbit that makes him a fascinating person to talk to. It's not always something heavy, and we certainly don't always see things the same way, but I actually enjoy asking him about things. Sometimes he throws in some pretty good advice too—even though I don't always use it!"*

*—Melanie*

Black men have an opinion on nearly everything. They have little difficulty sharing that opinion, given half a chance. They do so in barbershops, locker rooms, board rooms, and bedrooms, among other places. Take note: They don't require that others agree with their opinion, but they greatly desire it be heard and respected.

Asking his opinion and valuing it is a very important way you make love to the intellectual part of your man. Unfortunately, outside of his relationships with the women who love him, what he thinks is often not sought or seriously considered. When you pursue his opinions, and truly listen to them, you touch a vital nerve in him.

Because a Black man can be so passionate, and sometimes even forceful in expressing his opinions, you may think he is demanding that you adopt his point of view. Not necessarily. Asking his opinion doesn't mean you don't have a valid one of your own. Respecting his doesn't require changing yours.

Let's not get too deep here. We're not just talking about his opinion on major issues of global significance. No, I also mean simple, stupid stuff too, like "What movie should we see?" "Do you like this blouse or the green one?" "Who do think should apologize, me or your mother?"

The content of his opinion is of less importance than the process of seeking, hearing, and affirming his right to have and share an opinion. You breathe new life into his self-esteem when you do so.

Let your conversation be filled with lots of "So what do you think about such-and-such . . . ?" In this way, you demonstrate just how much you value his thoughts, and how much you value him as well.

**Say it:** "I honor the man that I love when I give his opinion two precious gifts—my attention and my consideration."

**Do it:** Ask him to detail what it means to him for you to solicit and value his opinion on matters both serious and silly. Tell him specific occasions in the past when he offered you an opinion that impressed, enlightened, or touched you!

# *33.* ▲ ■ ◆ *If You're a Talker, Listen Up*

*"I'd get jealous and very offended every time it happened. Gregory wouldn't have two words to say to me at home. Then I'd hear him on the telephone with one of his buddies talking and laughing—sometimes for an hour or more. What would really get my goat is when he would tell them things about his day, or something funny that happened, or even something that may have been bugging him—and it would be things he hadn't told me anything about. He'd be right there running it all down to his friends with lots of detail and plenty of enthusiasm. I didn't mind him telling them, I just wished he would talk that way to me too. One day at lunch, I was going on and on complaining about it to my girlfriend Doreen. She turns to me and says, with this big 'I'm smiling, but I'm not joking' look, 'Girl, have you ever considered that maybe the man doesn't talk to you because you don't give anybody a chance to get a word in edgewise?' "*

*—Belinda*

Are you one of those people for whom talking is an art form? You love to shape your ideas, choose your words, and speak your mind. You adore the sound of your own voice as much as the sound of Whitney's, Anita's, or Patti's. Verbalizing where you are coming from on a given issue—great or small—is something you approach with creativity and confidence. You are by nature a talker, and listening may be a skill that you need to sharpen. It's easy to stick with what you do well and ignore what you don't. That should be especially avoided in the area of communicating.

Like it or not, the very nature of effective communication requires that you both talk well and listen well. It's not even possible to develop an emotionally intimate relationship unless both of you talk up *and* listen up.

If you are a talker, you may sometimes get the impression that the man in your life resents your ease and ability with words. If you look closer, you may find that he has little trouble with how you talk to him, but lots of trouble with how you don't listen.

Black men long to be heard and understood by their women. It's a big part of filling their respect reservoirs. Serious listening is the only way to get good understanding. Serious listening requires you fight off all those inner urges to do other kinds of business while he's trying to talk to you. Business like:

- Silently rehearsing what you plan to say when it's your turn to speak again.
- Assuming you already know what he's about to say, and playing deaf until it's your turn to speak again.
- Focusing your attention elsewhere (on the TV, out the window, on the kids) until it's your turn to speak again.

Listening is by no means passive. When you are truly listening, you will offer more than just your open ears. When you do it right you fully engage your whole being in understanding your man's message and the feelings that motivated it. An active listener will:

- Invite him to talk about it, by simply promising, "I'm listening . . ." then really do it.
- Ask questions about what he said to get clarity.
- Repeat what you understood him to have said to assure accuracy.
- Use generous amounts of nods, uh-huhs, okay, touches, and other "I'm listening" signals.

If you're a talker, you want to be listened to. The best way to ensure that happening is by committing to listening to him when he speaks. The more deposits you make when you're the listener, the more withdrawals you can make when you're the talker.

**Say it:** For reasons that I hope are very obvious, there is no "Say it" for this chapter. Shh . . . !

**Do it:** Have someone read this section aloud to you. Only listen. Don't prepare a response. Just listen, and really hear it.

# 34. •❯ *If You're a Listener, Speak Up*

*"What I really hate the most is to be out with a guy, like at a restaurant or somewhere, and he's doing just fine at carrying the conversation. Very interesting and talkative. I'll be across the table, throwing in my perfectly timed 'Is that right's, 'Really's, or 'I didn't know that's. With my shy self, it never fails. As soon as I get good and relaxed, he'll say, 'Now you talk, tell me about you.' That's when I nearly choke and feel like I can't put three words together right."*

*—Christina*

If, in the company of the Black man in your life, you find yourself mostly soaking up his words of wit and wisdom, digesting his dialogue, and contemplating his conversation—you're a listener. That means you probably know his opinions, experiences, and feelings very well. It could also mean he doesn't know yours much at all.

Silence is golden, but speaking up is equally valuable. You need both precious commodities. Whatever your reasons, if you're too much with the ears and too little with the tongue, you need to strike a new balance.

In order to have an intimate relationship with you, the man in your life definitely needs to know you. He needs to know what occupies your thoughts, dreams, and fears. He needs to know your favorite Jackson 5 song, your best Christmas, your biggest frustrations, and your fondest ambitions. He needs to know the way your mind and heart work, what troubles them and what eases them.

The real difficulty with him getting those goodies is that no matter what kind of positive ID, high-level security clearance badge, or secret access code he may have to you, he can't get to know the inside of you unless you take him on a guided tour. Really talking to him, not just listening with an occasional question, is the way you take him there.

If you are shy, soft-spoken, and intimidated by his verbal ability, remember you don't have to speak up as well as he does. He is not your opponent in a debate. He's your lover. Share yourself with him by your words. You'll get better at talking, by talking; and he'll get better at listening by having to.

A major part of loving him is giving him the chance to really know and love you. Talk to him.

**Say it:** "Neither fear nor my natural quietness will keep me from sharing myself with the man I love. I have listened and shall continue. I shall speak up also, and I will continue to, for his sake and mine."

**Do it:** Role-play with your man. Have him do an exaggerated version of your normal conversational style, and you his, for an evening. Afterward talk together about how it felt and what, if any, changes in the talking/listening ratio between you should be made.

# 35. ▲ ■ ● ◆ ◗
## *Start with the Bottom Line, Then Add the Details*

*"It just kills me when he does that 'clock thing.' I'll be sitting there explaining something that's important to me, and his eyes are darting nervously to the clock on the wall, and he'll fidget with his hands or squirm impatiently in his seat. I'll be just pouring my heart out, truly hoping he's grasping the minute details of my*

*issue, when finally he'll interrupt me and ask, with this big confused look on his face, 'So what's your point?' "*

—*Helen*

Black men and the women who love them seem to come from two different planets when it comes to communication style. Women naturally build from the abstract to the concrete, the general to the specific. Men do just the opposite.

Communication is not about right ways or wrong ways. It's about effective ways or ineffective ones. Whatever works, works. With a Black man, getting to the "bottom line" first works.

Everyone wants to be heard—not just heard, but understood. Men hear and understand you best when they are confident they already know the point of what you're saying. When they don't hear it from you, they are apt to assume, filling in the blanks for themselves.

When they assume, they are apt to be wrong. The true meaning in your message then drifts away in a cloud of confusion.

You go through the effort to communicate something to your man, because that something is important to you. You trust that he will hear it, process it, understand it. You want him to "get it." So talk as long as you wish, be as articulate as you can— but remember, he's waiting to hear your "real" point. *Start with it.* For example: "I'd like to talk about how little time we've been spending with each other, because I want to see us increase it [your bottom-line point]. Now, let me tell how I've been feeling about this, and why . . . [the details]."

Start with the bottom line, then add the details. That way he will know where you are taking him in the world of ideas, and you will better ensure that your full message is heard (not always agreed with, but at least heard and understood). The quicker he knows where you are headed, the more likely he is to go there with you.

**Say it:** "I am not helpless in making myself heard and understood. The message I send has to do with how I am. The methods I use to get my message heard have to do with how he is."

**Do it:** Choose two fairly significant issues that you want to talk with him about. Share one of them, putting the bottom line last; then share the other, putting the bottom line first. In which conversation did you feel most completely heard and understood?

# 36. ▲ ■ ● ◆ ◗
## *Use "I" Statements*

*"We were sitting there talking and out of nowhere, with this big innocent grin on his face, Cory says to me, 'Keisha, you have an amazing talent. You know how to talk for hours, and when you finish you still haven't let it be known what you think or how you feel about whatever we were talking about.'"*

*—Keisha*

The Black man you love will be better off the sooner he accepts the fact that you are the world's leading expert on the subject of you. And you will be better off the sooner you begin to speak and act as though you have accepted that fact too.

Statements that start with "I ..." use more vowels, consonants, and syllables to talk about what's going on with you than what is, isn't, or should be going on with him. "I" statements are like opening your autobiography for him to read and learn about you. Statements that start with "You ..." are like scanning his, and telling him how to rewrite it.

Trade in your "You" statements, which include, "You ought to ..." "You did/didn't ..." "You should have ..." "You knew better ..." "You" statements bump you up a notch or two above him, which separates you from him. "You" statements promote defensiveness, frustration, and isolation.

In exchange for a mouthful of worthless "You" statements, you can pick up unlimited quantities of valuable "I" statements, like "I see that ..." "I think ..." "I feel ..." "I want ..." "I will ..." These help the man you love to hear, understand, and respond to what's going on with you.

To be sure, it is easier to give expert commentary on someone else than to take the risk of sharing your own insides. Talking about yourself makes you vulnerable; you run the risk of having your words ignored, scorned or confused. To talk in "I" invites the possibility of rejection. But risk it—you must for the sake of intimacy between you.

To talk about you and your feelings is neither self-centered nor egotistical. The most important information you can give your mate is your own truthful self-disclosure. He can only get that from you. "I" statements help you to give it to him.

**Say it:** "Neither the word 'I' nor the statements I make that begin with it are something to be afraid of. This simple word helps me give him a guided tour inside my soul."

**Do it:** Practice "I" statements. Make an earnest attempt for the next several days to refrain from starting any sentence with the word "You." Speak on the same subjects you normally would, but start with "I." For example, instead of "You should always open the car door for me when we go out. You know that!" try, "I really love it when you open the car door for me. I feel very special and very impressed."

# 37. ■ ◆ ◗ *Avoid "Never" and "Always"*

*"To tell you the truth, I don't really remember what we were arguing about. But I'm sure it was one of those times when he said he'd do something, and then he didn't do it—or didn't do it the way he said he would. Whatever it was about wasn't as important to me as the fact that it had happened again. As usual, I was fussing about this being the 'fifty-'leventh' time, and how he always manages to disappoint me and never does what he says he's going to do. And as usual, Ralph*

*was accusing me of being all black or white, never seeing the gray areas, and always side-stepping his positives to get to the negatives."*

*—Irma*

"Never" and "always" are the two words in the English language that appear almost exclusively in the context of either a blatant exaggeration, or an outright lie. For example: "You never show me any affection" or "You always have something else on your mind when I'm talking to you." "Never" and "always" seldom accurately describe any human being's behavior.

Think about the man you love, or the ones you have loved. They have their share of strengths and weaknesses, fine points and flaws. Imperfect human beings are very unlikely to have a perfect record at anything—good or bad. We don't "never" or "always" anything. To say we do is either an unrealistic indictment or unwarranted praise. In a relationship with a Black man your use of the two words should be avoided altogether.

Your use of "never" and "always," whether in condemnation or commendation, falls short of reality. It also diminishes the value of the times that he does what you say he never does, or didn't do what you say he always does.

If he sees that you grade only Pass/Fail, all or nothing, his incentive to do whatever it is more often will be dramatically lessened. All-or-nothing standards make it too easy to totally flunk. To his ears your "never" or "always" sound like you give no credit for "sometimes," "every now and then," or "once or twice . . ."

Good substitutes for "you never" and "you always" are "Rarely do you . . ." or "A lot of times you . . ." If you put your mind to it you can come up with some others that work as well. In any case, never say "never" and always avoid "always."

**Say it:** "I hereby call a halt to the use of 'never' and 'always' statements in my relationship. I now surrender all of my old, stored-up ones, trading them in for some shiny new 'sometimes,' 'seldom,' and 'frequently.'"

**Do it:** Commit to using "never" and "always" in the same way that you use your furnace in July.

# 38. ■ ◆ *Praise in Public, Protest in Private*

*"I remember when we were all in college together. John and I would double-date with Vernon and Janette all the time. What stands out most in my memory is how ridiculously in love Vernon and Janette were. They were always hand-holding and cuddling and kissing—they couldn't keep their hands off each other. But more than that, the way they talked to each other was so cute. When we were out together, every little thing Vernon did was followed by Janette's breathless, high-pitched 'Oh Vernon that was so wonderful.' We used to tease her behind her back, saying, 'If Vernon picked his nose, Janette would just swoon and say "Oh Vernon that was so wonderful . . ." ' He just loved it too. That's why it's so sad, now that they are married, Janette never has anything good to say about Vernon—and if she does, she doesn't say it around him. Many times I've gotten embarrassed when we're all out somewhere and Janette will start in on Vernon about something he should've done. It doesn't matter if a million people are around. When Janette gets ready to jump on him about something she does it, no matter where they are. She just dogs him out. I get so embarrassed for him. I guess Vernon is not so wonderful to her anymore. I'm pretty sure Janette is not that wonderful in Vernon's eyes either."*

*—Carol*

The quickest way to kill a relationship with a Black man is to embarrass, berate, criticize, lambaste, or otherwise "dis" him in public. To have a beef with him is fine, to serve it up in the presence of others is not.

You may well ask, "Why must Black men have such fragile egos? Aren't they tough enough to take a few words from little ole me?" For him, it's not about ego and toughness. It's about time and place. To protest something he did, didn't do, should have done, said, felt, or been in public is neither the right time nor place.

Much of the Black man's innate sense of pride and dignity is tied to the public image he and his woman project together. With a few choice words at the wrong time, you have the ability to broadcast to a watching world glaring deficiencies between him and you. To him, it is critical that he can depend on you not to air your relationship's dirty laundry where others may see it.

"In public" can be defined as anytime there is someone, other than the two of you, in eye or earshot. When in public, devote yourself to expressing to him, and others, whatever positive words of praise he may be due, however many or few.

Obviously, "in private" is when you and he are completely alone. There, with all sincerity and detail, protest as needed (of course, praise works well in private too).

To insist upon public protest is to be motivated by a desire to employ the sting of shame and embarrassment in order to correct a matter. That's playing dirty. Clean up your act.

**Say it:** "Our public times give me the opportunity to pay him tribute in word and deed. Our private times, to voice my protest. I will handle both with great care."

**Do it:** Before you go out in public together, think of three sincere words of praise to share with him. While you are out, drop one on him. Watch closely and notice the positive effect your praise has on him, and on the two of you together. (Helpful hint: With men, positive feelings are often expressed nonverbally or indirectly.)

# 39. ■ ◆ ◗ *Brag About Him, in Front of Him*

*"We had gone to a big Fourth of July barbecue at our neighbors' house. Johnny and I both had had a good time, laughing, talking, and eating with all the others. Around six o'clock or so, I could tell Johnny was ready to go. He's one of those people who decide to go one second and is out the door the next. I'm not like that. I like to go around hugging and kissing, exchanging phone numbers and making lunch dates, as we gradually leave. So, I kid you not, Johnnny was standing behind me literally pushing me toward the door, with his hands around my waist. Every time I stopped to say a quick goodbye to somebody, I could hear Johnny groan and whisper, 'Come on baby, let's go, we're never going to get out of here.' We were at the door, and stopped to thank our hosts. I just knew if I lingered much longer Johnny would have a stroke or something—he was already acting like he had to pee. Bobette and Jerry complimented me on the baked beans we had brought. Well, I proudly told them that Johnny had fixed them, and started bragging about how great a cook he is. I told them how wonderful it is to come home to one of Johnny's gourmet meals that he whips up to surprise me. I was boasting, and I knew it, so did Johnny. He was so proud, he was blushing. After all his rushing me, we stood in that doorway for almost thirty minutes while Johnny gave Bobette recipes and cooking tips. I thought we'd never leave."*

*—Marla*

Bragging, boasting, flaunting, and showing off are the perfectly harmless, though admittedly obnoxious, ways a Black man points a finger at himself and says admiringly, "Ain't I something!" Just as male peacocks strut their colors, and male lions proudly display their manes, Black men brag. It's a self-congratulatory "man-thang."

Bragging is nourishing to his ego in ways that may be hard for you to comprehend. When he boasts about himself, he's actually less concerned with what the hearer thinks than he is with what he thinks about himself. Men remind themselves of their own significance by bragging. Every boast is a dose of fresh self-affirmation.

An advanced-level skill in loving a Black man involves your knowing how to brag about him to others while in his listening range.

The women who love Black men rack up huge bonus points when they verbalize how much they are genuinely impressed with something about him. Take the time and make the effort to let his friends and family, and yours, know something you find "simply wonderful" about him while he looks on. This is music to his ears. It's no superficial sound bite, but a highly meaningful intimacy connection between you and your man.

You don't have to go out of your way to brag about him, or awkwardly try to force a boast into the conversation. What it takes is having, in the front of your mind, the things you really love and appreciate about who he is and how he is. Then, whenever he's around, and you get half a chance let one or two of them fall trippingly from your lips. When you do, look closely and you will notice his chest expand, his chin lift, and his feet just about rise off the ground.

**Say it:** "I don't have to wait for an opportunity to build up the man I love—I make the opportunities. Even if no other person on earth boasts about him, I will; and I will let him hear me do it."

**Do it:** Stop and think about some creative ways to brag about your man that are natural and sincere. One example is to simply introduce him to others by saying something along these lines, "I'd like you to meet my gorgeous and incredibly romantic husband/boyfriend/mate, Bill . . ."

# 40. ▲ ■ ● ◆ ◗ *Touch Him, Often*

*"We can be watching TV, going somewhere in the car, or even lying in bed, and Leonard will just reach over, without a word, pick up my hand and rest it on his thigh. I may be in the middle of a sentence or even half-asleep—but that doesn't stop him. As soon as my hand is settled on him he gets this look, like everything in the world is just fine with him. It's a funny little habit, but I love when he does it. It's the most hilarious thing to look over and see my big, buff, two-hundred-pound cop beam just because I've touched him."*

*—Lavette*

Sometimes words fail you. At those moments you can't seem to summon the vocabulary, grammar, syntax—or the time—to convey to him your most powerful emotions and affections. You can't go wrong if you touch him.

Touching delivers so many intimate messages. It calms, reassures, encourages, grants forgiveness, and starts a brand-new page in the history of your relationship.

Even if you never hear them say so, men cherish your touch. Touching sends the message that you are truly present with them. When you spontaneously touch him as you speak or listen, as you feel hurt or soothe his, as you ponder, decide, or work it out, you are very effectively closing up some of the tiny gaps that day-to-day living can make between you and your man. Nothing that costs so little has ever yielded so much.

I'm talking here about your basic, uncomplicated, reach-out-and-touch. Caressing, stroking, and fondling are fine, and not to be avoided. But I am attempting to sell you on the liberal use of plain, garden-variety touch.

Black men are well aware that you won't reach out to touch what you find distasteful or unappealing. He knows you touch what you treasure, not to restrain or rearrange it, but to experience the momentary pleasure of handling what you find precious.

Your touch validates him, and in an instant, reaffirms the fact that he is precious cargo in your world.

**Say it:** "I am never without some means of communicating my love to my man. What's in my heart can be effectively conveyed through my hands."

**Do it:** Take a week to experiment with simple touch with the man in your life, or other people you care about. Try one-handed, two-handed, light touch or heavier strokes. Develop a personal repertoire. Be aware of actually trying to "say something" by your touch. In seven days, ask the "touchee" if he noticed, and what it meant to him.

# 41. ▲■●◆) *Laugh with Him*

*"We had both been under quite a bit of strain for several months by then. His company was threatening to lay him off, we had the new baby, and our IRS problems were working our nerves raw. By the time we got home most evenings we were a pretty dreary-looking couple, with little to say and next to nothing to laugh about. Nothing in our lives seemed very funny at the time. One night at dinner, we tried to make cheerful conversation with each other and, as usual, we hadn't gotten very far. Larry finished eating and went into the den. I thought he'd be watching television or moaning and groaning over some of the bills or tax stuff, and finally go to bed. Ten minutes after he left the table, Larry had turned the stereo up to blasting and was playing—of all things—some silly old disco album. When I went into the den to see what had gotten into him, I could not believe my*

*eyes. Larry had put on his old* Saturday Night Fever *polyester suit and those beat-up platform shoes he's always kept in the back of the closet. He saw me peek in, and without a word, he went into his best* Soul Train *line dance steps. I mean he was acting like a fool, trying to get a laugh out of me. When I saw all that, I lost it. I laughed until tears came down my cheeks. Both of us did. For that entire night, every time we looked at each other we would laugh hysterically. It was the most fun we had had in a very long time."*

*—Willa*

If everything about love were life-or-death serious then nobody would be able to stand more than ten minutes of the stuff. Maybe we've let relationships get too complicated. We trudge right past the fun and foolishness that love used to have. Lighten up.

Black men and the women who love them are different enough, and life and love are complicated enough, to keep you working hard and sweaty just trying to be happy. Don't let love become a set of rules and regulations, and time together just another earnest attempt to crack each other's code. Lots of somewheres along the way, laugh with each other.

Grins, giggles, and polite chuckles are fine, but you can do better than that. You and your man, at least once a day, need to throw back your heads and laugh till your noses flare, your jaws ache, and your eyes water.

I don't want to be guilty of minimizing the seriousness of love, or of trivializing the challenges that may exist in your relationship. And, no, I am sure I don't know what you and he have been going through lately. Perhaps if I did, I'd sit right down and cry a river for you. But surely if you took a look at the two of you, daily trying so hard to stay "the two of you," you'd find something to lie down on the floor and laugh about. Do it together.

Finding each other, loving each other, and changing with each other is very hard work, full of unexpected twists, turns, and detours. It's also full of humor, even hilarity, if you look for it.

Your laughter mingling with his is a most passionate form of lovemaking. Keep it both frequent and intense. Let yourself go.

**Say it:** "Laughter doesn't change the circumstances of my life, it changes me. I make a new commitment to pursue laughter as a regular part of my love."

**Do it:** During the last twenty-four hours where was there rich humor that you could have embraced and didn't? Recount the experience to a friend or lover and take the time to give it the laughter it deserves. Try to remember the way you used to laugh when you were ten years old and hadn't yet learned about being dignified, serious-minded, and ladylike. Laugh again.

# 42. ▲ ■ ● ◆ ◗ *Pray for Him, Pray with Him*

*"There's a certain look Stan gets on his face. He's usually very quiet and doesn't say a word; but I can see it in his face and in his whole body. It's the look of discouragement. Sometimes I know what's bothering him—too much month and not enough money, or some pressure from the job, or just the feeling of not being able to do anything to make his ambitions happen quicker. Stan feels like giving up sometimes and it hurts me to see him that way. I want so badly to do something or say something to help. That's when I remember my grandmother's response to nearly any problem. She'd say, 'Baby, you'd better tell God about it.'"*

*—Edna*

Love is something that comes straight from the heart of God. To fail to experience love's spiritual dimension is to settle for quite a shallow kind of love. There is no way to disconnect God from real love; after all, love was His great idea in the first place. But it is possible to ignore His role in your daily effort to sustain your love.

Prayer is not only the act of talking to God, it is also an attitude of trusting in God. Trusting Him to be on the listening end, anxious to respond out of His love and power. Isn't that just what the man you love needs, the love and power of God at work in his life? When you pray with him, or for him, you ask for it on his behalf.

Face it. You really don't have, in your hands, everything it takes to cultivate lasting, mutually satisfying love. It takes resources far beyong the visible, tangible, and humanly obtainable to make the miracle of loving relationships happen. Prayer is your access to the God who holds and dispenses those resources.

Regularly take time to pray with, and for, the man you love. Pray until it becomes as natural as date-making and hand-holding. There is nothing you can do with the man you love that is more intimate than to pray. We talk to God about that which is most important to us in all the world. When you pray with, and for, the man you love, you hear from each other's mouths what your most profound yearnings are for each other.

**Say it:** "The man in my life, and my love for him, matter to me and to God. Why would I not talk to the God of the universe about what matters most to me?"

**Do it:** Together (if he will) or alone (if he won't) establish a regular time of conversation with God especially about your relationship. Brief and simple works very well. Be patient with yourselves, but stay committed to making prayer with and for him a consistent part of your life.

# 43. ▲ ◆ *Allow Him to Keep Some Secrets, Allow Yourself*

*"I want to know all about Victor, and I want him to know all about me, every detail of my life. I have nothing to hide. Why would we hold anything back, if we say we really love each other? That's how I see it, anyway. Of course, Victor doesn't see it that way at all."*

—*Lynette*

An important aspect of what makes individuals individual is their secrets. Secret-keeping, in and of itself, is neither shameful nor harmful. To have some secrets that stay secret is not illegal. It breaks no real law of love.

The man you love descends from a long line of Black men who have not always been allowed to have and to hold what rightly belongs to them. Your man is the son, grandson, and great-grandson of proud patriarchs who felt the humiliating sting of having what should have been their own taken by brute force. Their land, their homes, their women and children, the fruit of their creativity and labor, the sense of power that is found in ownership. Your man always shares his forebears' grief and sometimes their experience too. His secrets may be among the only possessions he can reserve as his, and his alone.

Black folk are very resistant to being probed ("getting in my business"). Men, in particular, don't want to be treated like baseball cards—a handsome picture on the front, and all his vital statistics on full display in the back.

Both of you need your share of secret thoughts, desires, and experiences. You need a private world. Men are usually quite determined to stand guard over theirs. Real love is a curious mixture of both intimacy and privacy, "us-ness" and "me-ness."

WARNING! DISCLAIMER! CAVEAT!: Secrets that keep you from knowing who your man really is (not merely what he's done and with whom, where he's been and with whom, how much, how little, how long . . . ) will definitely inhibit the growth of soul-sharing love. I'm advocating a little harmless secret-keeping, not deceptions and failure to self-disclose. That's "hiding out," not secret-keeping. Hiding out is unacceptable.

Knowing everything about your partner is not nearly as critical as knowing the important parts of who he is—his hurts, struggles, desires, yearnings, fears, and values—the things that inhabit his guts. These secrets you must know and you must share. At the right time, with all the wisdom and courage you can muster, tell him those vital secrets, and request them from him. Don't push, don't pry, and don't give up!

For you to allow your man to legitimately have a private world makes him much more likely to invite you into it.

**Say it:** "I choose to respect and protect his (and my) right to hold some things secret. It is healthy. At the same time, I choose not to be a party to keeping secrets that keep us from really knowing each other. It is unhealthy and results in counterfeit intimacy."

**Do it:** Share this chapter with the Black man you love. Talk together about what kinds of secrets each of you consider healthy and the kinds that are unhealthy. Be specific. Promise not to fret about the former, and to not withhold the latter.

# 44. ▲ ■ ● ◆ *Stay Out of His Stuff*

*"It was right during the time when our relationship began to get kind of serious, and we started using words like 'our future together,' 'marriage,' 'children,' and 'our home' a lot. Knowing everything about him seemed so much more important than it had before. I had to make sure that I had a pretty thorough 'file' on him before I got too deeply committed. I began to glance a little longer at his stack of mail whenever he laid it down, and to listen a little more closely when he would replay his answering machine messages. At first, it seemed kind of funny how nosy you can get and how your mind can run away with all kinds of suspicions. It stopped being funny when I happened to find his private journal lying out on his desk. The thing was almost calling out my name. I was just a heartbeat away from picking it up and browsing through, before I caught myself. There would've been no way in the world to explain my way out of that one."*

*—Kelly*

This point may seem too obvious to even warrant space in this book. You would think that everybody knows to stay out of everybody else's stuff. You would think.

Prying, poking, snooping, opening, searching, and sneaking into are some of the most dangerous and undignified acts any woman can commit. Men hate that some women choose to do it, and the women who love them hate what they uncover when they do it. It's bad news for both of you.

When uninvited, stay out of his drawers, closets, pockets, papers, and cabinets. If you feel it's the only way to get to the real truth, that's a sure sign the relationship lacks honesty, trust, and mutual respect in the first place. Whatever it is you may find is not going to make things any better—and probably a whole lot worse!

Getting to the truth is important, but how you get to it is equally important. Whether it's your hands, eyes, ears, or nose in his stuff (or his in yours), we're talking about a serious violation of someone else's space. It has no place in a loving relationship.

Because you wouldn't want, under any circumstances, to admit that you went through his stuff, you will never be in the position to get absolute confirmation that what you found is what you think it is, or means what you think it means. No man, guilty or innocent, will feel obligated to explain evidence gotten through snooping. If you find nothing, you will have to live with the guilt of having betrayed his trust in you. If you do find something, you are now no less guilty of a crime than you may suppose him to be.

Snooping is a fear-based response. It demeans and devalues the one who does it and the relationship itself. It proceeds from a position of weakness and desperation, rather than strength and assertiveness. It reduces the most refined and intelligent women, instantly transforming them into unappealing blobs of paranoia.

Keep your eyes open and ask for honest answers to your honest questions. Draw conclusions and make decisions based on information you have gotten by legitimate means. Trust yourself enough to be able to do what you need to do with what you've gotten rightly. If you go looking for dirt, you are liable to find it, and it's liable to get all over you.

**Say it:** "Respect for his privacy and possessions is reason enough for me to stay out of his stuff. Respect for myself is an even better reason."

**Do it:** Congratulate yourself, either because you've never been guilty of snooping, or because you won't ever be again.

# 45. ▲ ● ◗ *Be His Partner, Not His Mother*

*"When I was a little girl, I loved to bring home stray cats, hungry dogs, and grounded pigeons. I got such a kick out of dressing their wounds and nursing them back to health. Then I hated it when, after I had taken such good care of them, I had to let them go. This was about the same time that I started letting Darnell, the boy who sat right behind me in the fifth grade, copy from my test papers. I didn't stop even after we got caught, because Darnell would look real pitiful at me and then he'd be so appreciative. I was hooked. I've got to pull myself together, though. I left the fifth grade over twenty years ago and I still find myself taking care of too many men who need to be taking care of themselves."*

*—Portia*

Every man on this planet, including your man, has but one mother. Perhaps she did a good job with him, perhaps not. You may know his mother well or may never have laid eyes on her. Of one fact you can be sure: He's got a mother, and it's not you.

Playing the role of Mama in your man's life keeps the two of you from ever knowing the rich satisfaction of love between two adults.

All in the name of love, women who play Mama:

- Subtly and overtly encourage men to believe that they need her, and for his own good should obey her too.
- Make it clear that she's willing and available to clean up all his messes and take complete responsibility for his care and well-being.

- Stay up at night crying over her "little boy" 's misdeeds.
- Do whatever it takes to keep him from suffering the consequences of his own choices.

Partners, on the other hand, are committed to what's healthy and empowering for each other, not just what's easiest.

Pull off your apron, put away your broom, and by all means reclaim your checkbook and credit cards from him. He doesn't need a mother standing over him; he needs a lover standing by him. If you are filling in for Mama, you are an impostor—and probably an exhausted one.

The woman who gives "Mama love" is selfishly trying to "raise" the kind of man that fits her standards and desires. At the same time she has come to believe that the only way she can keep him is to mother him. And since she thinks she must have him, at all costs, she keeps right on mothering, in spite of the disastrous results.

Men despise dependence. They treasure autonomy and self-sufficiency. The very thing she fears is exactly what she is setting herself up for. Because, although some men will temporarily accept Mama love, they will also resent it—and the woman who gives it.

If you keep playing "Mama-who-runs-to-the-rescue," he'll keep playing "Irresponsible-little-boy-in-a-jam." Eventually a brutal and intractable law of nature comes into play: LITTLE BOYS GROW UP AND LEAVE THEIR MAMAS . . .

**Say it:** "Boys will be boys and men must be men. I must be his lover, and not his mother. There is no way can I honestly be both."

**Do it:** Make a thorough and specific list of the things you do for him that you suspect are more like mothering than partnering. For each behavior on your list, set a target date to stop providing that caretaking service. One item at a time, tell the man in your life, the date (within days or weeks, not years!) that you will cease to perform that function. In spite of his objections, or your own resistance, on that date stop. Move on to the next item and repeat the process.

# 46. ▲❯ *Be His Lover, Not His Toy*

*"Dwayne's point is that he and Kimberly are still very good friends, even though
they aren't involved anymore. I'm supposed to understand that they have this deep
spiritual bond between them that will always be there, and it has nothing to do
with romantic or sexual attraction. He says he's serious about a future with me,
but that I'm way too insecure, if I'm not going to be able to handle him talking to
Kimberly on the phone every day. Plus, they have to be able to get together for these
long private lunches, to which I am not invited, every couple of weeks. Dwayne
kept telling me that their friendship is no threat to our relationship, and that I
needed to back off it. I must have started to believe him, because I was feeling silly
about complaining so much and was trying to accept their friendship as best I
could. I was learning to live with it, until last night, when Dwayne told me that he
wouldn't be able to go with me today to check out a reception hall for our
wedding. His friend, Kimberly, is going through some big crisis with her boyfriend
and she needs Dwayne to help her 'sort things out.' I'm sorry, I have to believe that
I am not supposed to have to deal with this kind of crap ... Right?"*

*—Shelley*

Have you ever heard yourself say something like "What I'm really looking for in
a relationship is a man who will carelessly toy with my mind, my body, my emotions,
and my time? He'll pull me down from my place on his shelf when he feels like it,
play with me to his heart's content, then toss me in a corner until he wants to play
with me again." Of course no woman has ever said that, but unfortunately there are
some who have ended up as some Boy Toy anyway. Don't let it happen to you.

The best way to ensure you stay off anyone's plaything list is for you to set and maintain clear personal boundaries—even at the risk of upsetting the relationship.

Boundaries are the limits that mark just how far you will allow yourself to be taken lightly and toyed with before you call a halt to it. It involves limits like how many times you will be told 7:00 and be picked up at 9:00, with no explanation, let alone apology. Or . . .

- how many lies and deceptions you'll catch him in, before you say (and mean) "No more."
- how much of your money is too much of your money to dole out and never see return.
- how many times you will let him show up, get in, and get over, when you had said, "No, not tonight."
- how many of his empty promises about stopping, starting, changing, or committing will you talk yourself into believing—one more time?

Ultimately, boundary-setting is simply getting accustomed to saying NO, not necessarily happy about it, or comfortable with it, but accustomed to it. For a veteran Boy Toy, "no" won't do. I'm talking, "NO!!!"

You'd be suffering from paranoia to assume that all Black men want to treat you like an occupant of their toy box. Most men aren't that vain, superficial, or arrogant. But some of them are, and you'd be naive to assume they aren't.

Women who play Barbie do so because, to them, being played with is better than never getting any play at all. They allow themselves to be handled like no more than a toy, because when you have low standards for yourself you set few boundaries for yourself. You'll never get any more than the kind of love you think you deserve.

If there's some Barbie in you, learning to say "NO!" (and mean it) and becoming a lover, not a toy, will be hard to do. It's even harder to keep on doing it (when the heat is on you'll be tempted to go back to your old ways). I can assure you, however, you will be enormously proud of yourself if you keep at it.

It will help you tremendously to bear in mind this time-tested truth: BOYS EVENTUALLY GET BORED WITH THEIR PLAYTHINGS and do one of two things: (a) They put their toy back on the shelf and go off searching for a shinier, newer one. (b) They break them open to explore their parts, and are soon trampling on the scattered innards. In either case, you'll have to admit things don't work out too well for the toy!

**Say it:** "I am the boundary keeper. I am the one who keeps me from being toyed with. I'd rather be alone now and a lover later, than to be a toy to be played with."

**Do it:** In real-life situations at home, work, with friends or your lover, practice boundary-setting by saying "NO!" when that's what you mean. Do it in spite of how you feel, or what it may cost. Resist the urge to give excuses, unnecessary explanations, and justifications. When necessary, in the name of self-respect, simply say "No." For the next few weeks, give yourself two points when you do it without defending or apologizing for it, otherwise give yourself one point. When you get twenty points, reward yourself with something wonderful.

# 47. ▲ *Pursue Him Because You Want Him, Not Because You Need Him*

*"From the first day he started working there, every female in the place took notice. He really was a nice guy. No, more than that, he was a real sweetheart, a gentleman, and he was absolutely as fine as he could be—smooth dark skin, big broad shoulders, and a flawless smile. Plus, he spoke like he really had some sense. I was impressed—and I definitely was interested. But I tried to play it cool, hoping that just maybe he'd strike up a conversation with me and maybe ask me out, and just maybe I'd say yes. But every woman in that office was throwing herself at him, so I started feeling like "Little Miss Cool the Fool." Since Richard and I broke up, I had a lot of lonely Saturday nights, and I guess deep down I was afraid I was going to miss out now. Next thing you know I'm doing all these busybody little*

*maneuvers to get his attention—like I just had to have this man, or something—begging plain and simple."*

*—Karen*

Forget tradition, forget what Mama told you or what fear led you to believe. The truth of the matter is: THERE IS ABSOLUTELY NOTHING WRONG WITH YOU MAKING THE FIRST MOVE. But make that move because you want to, not because you've got to. You see him. You like him. You want him. You pursue him. Sometimes getting together will be because of your efforts. That's okay. Staying together will be because of both of you.

The most self-defeating misbelief that you could ever hold is that you need a man to call your own in order to survive. You need air. You need food. You need water. As desirable as being loved by a Black man may be, you don't need one to survive. If you think you do, you'll act accordingly. If you do that you'll cheapen your worth as an individual. And, if you do that you are living a miserable and tragic lie.

The love and companionship of a good Black man may be highly prized by you. You have great expectations of how you (and he) will be better for having come together. Acting upon a desire to have him in your life can have very constructive results. Acting upon a false sense of need to have him in your life is bound to lead to destructive ends.

The women who are happiest with their men are the ones who can also be happy without them. They recognize that a relationship with him enriches and embellishes her life. It doesn't give her life.

Go for him, but pursue him as you would pursue gold—in order to thrive—not in the way you'd pursue water—in order to survive!

**Say it:** "The steps that I take toward a Black man come from desire, not necessity. It is not feverish pursuit of what I need to have, but a deliberate advance toward who I want to have."

**Do it:** Talk to a few of your sister-friends about what the look, feel, and results of need-based love and desire-based love are. Apply rigorous honesty as you take stock of yourself on this issue.

# 48. ▲ ●
## *Get a Life of Your Own—*
## *Don't Borrow His*

*"When I was little, I thought my Aunt Estelle was so glamorous, rich, sure of herself, and that she knew something about almost everything. When she met Uncle Albert, she started acting differently. It was so strange to see somebody like her pretending that she really needed him to help her decide what to think, what to do, and how to act all the time. To be honest though, around men I sometimes catch myself acting just like Aunt Estelle."*

*—Celina*

You are a whole, complete, fully assembled human being. All of your parts work—or you've learned to live with the ones that don't! Neither the Black man you love, nor your relationship with him, give you an identity. You already have one. It has your name on it.

A loving relationship with a Black man should never mean you give up your unique personality. Who you are (and how you are) are much too important to let that happen. It's nice if he knows this; it's vital that you do. Loving him doesn't mean losing you.

Think about it. What we all want out of love is to be fully known (the good, the bad, and the ugly) and fully accepted. Careful. Don't seek the rewards of approval and miss the rewards of love. Refuse to say, do, or even think anything that is motivated solely by approval-seeking.

Imagine the Queen of Sheba abandoning her vast kingdom, or Nefertiti giving up her regal bearing, Harriet Tubman disposing of her courage, or Mary McLeod

Bethune hiding her brilliance. How about Maya Angelou putting down her pen, or Lena Horne camouflaging her grace and charm—all in the name of love. That's not love at all, it's suicide! The women who love Black men are daughters of these "she-roes." Who you are is too much to lose.

Never:

- lose touch with your own opinions, perspectives, and convictions. Declare them.
- hold your unique personality hostage. Display it.
- abandon your vision, goals, dreams. Pursue them.

Fear may tempt you to believe that unity and uniformity are synonymous. They are not.

Uniformity is a unity counterfeit that requires one of you to forfeit your uniqueness in order to become acceptably similar to the other person.

Unity is the miracle of two very different individuals with dissimilar backgrounds, tastes, experiences, and personalities choosing to commune together. Two who not only accept their uniqueness, but celebrate it.

The Black man you love gains little when he has you, but not the things that make you, you. Love him enough to love yourself enough to be the best of who you are.

Boldly offer your lover what you have already given a stamp of approval to—you.

**Say it:** "I am who I am. I don't have to be what I perceive he would approve of. That is a double-edged insult. Neither of us profits anything if I give up my life to gain his love."

**Do it:** Ask your most trusted and truthful sister-friends if they notice you being "less you" when you are with him, compared to when you are with them. Find out what parts of your speech, style, intellect, interests, or abilities have been safely locked away from his sight. Liberate them. If you've taken on his identity, or one he has fashioned for you—stop now. Return what you've borrowed of his. Get your life back!

# 49. Commit to Who He Is Now, Not Who You Hope He'll Become

*"I told him, 'I accept you just the way you are . . .' I guess what I really meant was, 'You'll change or I'll die trying to make you.'"*

—*Regina*

Loving your man's potential more than you love who he is now is relationship sabotage. Beware. You may be despising the frog, while waiting on the prince who may never appear. Take a good hard look at the man in your life, or the one trying to find his way in. You don't have to have a relationship with him if the way he is is not acceptable to you. But if you take him, take him because you can love him as he is today.

Don't deny or abandon your hopes for his positive personal development, or even future transformations in his life. "Change," "Improvement," and "Progress" are not four-letter words.

Do, however, recognize that change in another human being is something you may influence, but something you cannot produce. Him changing is up to him.

Black men (and every other variety of the human species) change and grow when they hunger for it, not when you (or anyone else) has that hunger for them. Ask and answer this crucial question: Can I, will I, love and live life with this man, if in all our tomorrows he stays exactly the way he is today?

Take a moment for an honest look inside. What do you really believe?

The Easy Lie: "I can love him enough to make him change."

Or

The Hard Truth: "I can love him enough that he feels free to choose to change."
The Easy Lie: "If I teach him a better way, he'll do it/say it/see it that way."

Or

The Hard Truth: "If I teach him a better way, he might not see it as better at all."

One of the paradoxes of real life is: Black men are most willing to "become" when they feel accepted as they come.

**Say it:** "I have every right to want what I want and who I want. But I have neither the ability nor the need to change him. I can choose to accept what he is today—and I reserve the right to choose not to (and move on)."

**Do it:** Ask yourself: "Do I take responsibility to make those I love change? When did I start? What motivates me to do that? What will I do about it?" Write it. Sign it. Do it.

# 50. Don't Make Him Pay for How Others Have Hurt You

*"I love Black men. I really do. But they have put me through so many changes, so many times. Now, as soon as one walks up I notice my smile is just a little slower, my expression a little stiffer. I may not even know this brother at all, but he reminds me of the others, and I feel that little kick in my stomach."*

*—Tamara*

It is absolutely impossible to love another human being without trusting him for something. Trust is woven into the very fabric of love.

Trust is counting on another's consistent willingness and ability to provide you the necessities that you treasure (support, respect, security, mutual affection, fairness, devotion). In the past, the one(s) you loved and trusted may not have given you that treasure, or they may have offered you some miserable substitute for it (such as rejection instead of support, abuse instead of respect, abandonment instead of concern). That is how you learned the gritty taste of pain in all its bitter flavors: disappointment, betrayal, victimization.

If you've ever loved deeply, you've trusted deeply. And, you're likely to have hurt deeply too. Old hurts can leave a constant, dull ache that perhaps you've "just learned to live with."

Examine yourself carefully. Are you:

- Suspicious?
- Jealous?
- Pretending?
- Hiding?
- Isolating?
- Withdrawing?

Is this the kind of treatment due the man in your life now? Or is he being punished for the sins of another? Hold him accountable for how he is, not how someone else was.

**Say it:** "I have loved, trusted, and hurt. All of these are my emotions. I own them. I can recover and even grow from my hurt. I will not deny, justify, or defend punishing my partner for how others have hurt me in the past."

**Do it:** Apologize. Make amends, with no requirements on what kind of response he must give.

# 51. ▲ ● ◆ *Take a Risk a Day (But Be No Fool)*

*"I haven't lived in L.A. all my life. I come from a tiny little town on the Gulf in Alabama. It is country with a capital C but it's where all my family is, and that means it's home. I lost my Southern drawl and small-town ways a long time ago—but I had never thought I was ashamed of my roots until last summer when my mother, father, and grandmother came out for a visit. I had just started going out with Vincent, and we were doing very well together. He always remarked that I was so classy and sophisticated and, at the same time, down-to-earth. I loved that image and I wanted very much for him to continue to think of me that way. I'm ashamed to admit it, but at first when my family came, I thought about keeping them from meeting Vincent. They're my people and I love them dearly, but they are very simple country people. They're loud and they love to crack jokes about how 'proper' I speak and act even though I come from Bon Secour, Alabama. They don't mean any harm, but they know how to seriously embarrass me. Letting them start that stuff with Vincent around seemed like too big a risk to our relationship at that stage. I guess I didn't want anything to change the classy image he had of me. Finally, though, I got my sanity back. I realized that if Vincent was really going to know who I was, he needed to understand where I come from. He would have to think what he wanted to think. I decided to take a chance and let him see the real deal; and I feel a whole lot better about myself for doing it."*

*—Cordelia*

Loving someone is risky business. Taking risks is scary because we are not absolutely sure what the outcome will be. There are, you may argue, so many ways to get hurt in relationships with Black men, and you may wonder "why in the world would I heighten the chances by taking any risks on purpose?" In loving, the failure to take calculated risks provides you a sense of safety and security. Too much safety and security keeps things the way they are—the boring, stagnant status quo—no growth, no progress, no change. It's a safe way to live, and it's a sorry way too.

Taking a risk a day involves stretching your limits, testing the possibilities, and walking through your fears. It's making wise choices about what the next courageous move is for you to make in a loving relationship with a Black man. It involves a willingness to put up something dear to yourself (like your time, your feelings, your insecurities, your ego) for a possible loss, or for the sake of great potential gain.

In your case, it may be as simple as mustering up the courage to speak to him where you've previously been silent. Or as complex as making a decision in your relationship that is as much from your heart as from your head. Risk-taking means daily taking another courageous step toward the kind of love—and lover—that you truly desire.

Risk-taking doesn't mean going for reckless, impulsive leaps off of love's diving board. That's being foolish and self-defeating. Rather, I am challenging you to "show up for your life," and cast off your procrastination and obsessive self-protection to do what feels right—if only you weren't so safe, secure, and terrified:

- Take the risk of letting some man see who you really are, behind the mask, and under your layers of protection.
- Take the risk of going for your first choice, rather than settling for your second, or third, or fourth . . .
- Take the risk of living as if what other people think about you is their business, and not yours at all.
- Take the risk of saying, "Yes. I think I will. I'm worth it." Or, "No more. I won't. I'm worth more than this."

The beauty of risk-taking is that some of your risks will return to you far more than you invested. Others may flop and go absolutely nowhere. Whichever the case, by taking the risk you will have strengthened your courage muscles just a little bit more.

**Say it:** "Too much safety and security can seduce me into stagnation. Stagnation is unacceptable to me. I want to reap the rewards that can only be mine by taking some wise risks today."

**Do it:** What is one necessary risk you must take to establish or enhance your relationship with the Black man you desire or already have? What is one risk-taking "baby-step" that you would take today, if only you weren't afraid? Take that step today anyway.

# 52. ■ ◆ *Behavior You Reward Is Behavior He Repeats*

*"It's always the same. I get on him real hard. He starts to do better, then he stops. Before you know it, he's gotten back into his old ways, worse than before. I feel like I've tried everything to get Brandon to see how he's messing up, and to get him to stop. It doesn't do any good. He just plain doesn't get it."*

*—Vanessa*

Whether he tells you so or not, your appraisal of his performance is more important to him than anyone else's. Every time you, in any way, communicate appreciation, acceptance, or approval of his actions you heighten the probability that he repeats that action.

Want him to be more affectionate, spontaneous, communicative? Pour on the praise when he does it. Don't just rush to criticize him when he doesn't. Criticism is easier, but far less effective than praise. Your expressions of approval are powerful incentives for him to do whatever he did, again and again.

All workers are motivated by a positive performance review and a generous paycheck. You are constantly in the position to provide the Black man you love dozens of minireviews and paydays everyday. What's payday for him assures a big payoff for you.

Is this manipulation? Absolutely not. It is your sincere, loving stamp of approval and appreciation of his relationship-enriching behaviors (emphasis on sincere).

Competency, accomplishment, effectiveness, and mastery are all powerful components of a Black man's self-identity. To him, what he does (and how well he does it) is inextricably tied to who he is. Rewarding his positive performance is a highly potent way of affirming his manhood.

Pepper your conversation with lots of "I love it so much when you . . ."

Be honest. Do you ever "reward" his negative behavior? By what you say, how you say it, or what you fail to say, have you inadvertently communicated approval of his inappropriate behaviors? Here too the principle applies: Behavior you reward is behavior he repeats.

**Say it:** "I lose nothing of who I am and what I have when I applaud my man's positive behaviors. I choose to give him what he may never get anywhere else—applause for his efforts at excellence."

**Do it:** Does the Black man in your life hear at least twice as many compliments as criticism from you? Make immediate adjustments accordingly.

# 53. ▲ ■ ● ◆ ◗ *Cry, but Never Whine*

*"I can't remember ever being any angrier at Sylvester than I was the time he called me a 'spoiled crybaby.' I was livid. Up until then, I knew that at times I would get teary-eyed if something upset me. I just thought it was one of the ways I coped with disappointments. To tell the truth, though, I had crossed the line with Sylvester. Sometimes I would boo-hoo and sling snot for days, because when I did he'd get busy doing what I wanted, how I wanted it."*

*—Varetta*

You have every right in the world to express whatever emotions you feel. In fact, most women understand that the shedding of tears is a perfectly acceptable and highly effective response to a wide range of emotions including sadness, joy, disappointment, fear, and surprise.

Black men do not always handle your tears as comfortably as you do. They are such "fixers," "solvers," and "producers" that they may struggle with the feeling that your tears mean he did something wrong—and that he is responsible for fixing it, ASAP. Because your man is so busy feeling guilty and responsible for doing something, he can't really tune in and support you fully in what you're going through. Your tears can really throw him off.

Cry anyway. Of course, it's healthy for you, but it's healthy for him as well. He will learn what tears mean and what they don't, and how to live more comfortably with them. Slowly but surely, he will "get it" as he discovers that your tears don't mean he must get busy repairing your life. Rather, it's his chance to join you in what's happening in your life at that moment.

A good, sincere cry is your body's way of paying tribute to what has already deeply touched your heart and soul. It's one of the most natural and honest human expressions. Though you expend effort and energy in doing it, crying is not meant to solve, settle, or signify anything. It's a "feeling thing," not a "fix-it thing." The man in your life might need your help understanding that.

Strategic crying is called whining. Whining is the shedding of tears and the manipulation of emotions done to solve, settle, or signify something. Whining is a fussy, inarticulate, and overly dramatic display by one lover meant to elicit some desired response from the other lover. Whenever your emotional expressions are meant to get something, or to change something outside yourself, you are whining.

Whining can get results—but only for a while. Beware. Black men detest the feeling of being "worked." Whining is an attempt to work him for your own purposes. Couple that with the fact that every time you whine he becomes a little less fazed by it and a little less impressed with you. Whining is the emotional equivalent of crying wolf; after a while, nobody pays attention anymore.

**Say it:** "I claim my tears, with no shame whatsoever. At the same time, I reject whining and all it stands for."

**Do it:** Knowing yourself the way you do, write your personal ten Commandments for avoiding whining and attempting more straightforward communication of emotional issues. (For example: "Thou shalt not direct thyself to cry on cue.")

# 54. ▲ ■ ● ◆ ) *Cry with Your Man*

*"I could not believe it ... talk about surprised—I was shocked. When I told Al that his nephew Kevin—his favorite nephew—I mean he has loved this boy like he was his own son. When I told him that Kevin had gotten into some kind of trouble and was calling from the police station, Al froze for just about a second like he was waiting for me to take back what I said. Then he finally stumbled to the phone, almost as if he wasn't really sure where to find it. If you had asked me before how I thought he would handle a crisis situation like this I would have predicted he would have picked up the phone, given Kevin the third degree, demanded to speak to whoever was in charge, and proceeded to rant and rave about racist cops and the unjust legal system, on and on. Loud and furious was what I would have expected—and all night long, at that. But after he hung up with Kevin, I came back into the room and Al was sitting on the edge of the bed staring straight ahead. When I looked closer, I saw huge tears streaming down his face. I could tell that he was so hurt and let down. I sat right next to him. I was so surprised to see him cry that way. I was literally speechless. Before you know it, we're both sitting there crying our eyes out. I held him tight, and we just cried."*

*—Barbara*

By now, I'm sure, everybody knows that real men do cry. Some do because they've stopped trying to hide their hurts so much. Others have always done it, but seldom let their women see them. Then, of course, there are those who recently started doing it because they think you like to see it every now and then. Whatever the reason, men are responsible for much more of the earth's saltwater content than ever before.

Black men's tears usually spring from a sense of being without control—that there is something in his life that he feels unable to fix, manage, or change. When he's in that space he feels vulnerable and more than a little lonely. Cry with him.

The absence of tears doesn't necessarily mean that your man is not feeling pain. But when he cries you can be assured that what he feels is very difficult for him.

When you cry with your partner you make it clear that you see his hurtful feelings as valid and his tears appropriate. In this very powerful way you minister to his vulnerability and his loneliness. You aren't, nor do you ever need to be, the solution for his pain, but you are support to him in bearing his emotional load.

Crying does not mean he's falling apart or cracking up. There is no need for you to rush to make him dry-eyed and happy again. That sends the message that you find something wrong with his expression of emotion. It speaks disapproval, and men covet your approval as fiercely as you covet their devotion.

Don't be afraid of his tears or yours. Let them flow freely. As your tears mingle together, weakness becomes strength, and misery does indeed love company.

**Say it:** "Whether the man I love is crying outwardly or inwardly, I choose to join him there. My love for him must make room for his tears as well as his laughter."

**Do it:** Finish this sentence: "When he's moved to tears the number one emotion I feel (or would feel) inside is _____." Is it sympathy, disgust, fear, respect, embarrassment, or something else? Does your feeling motivate you to cry with him, or pull away from him? If the emotion is one that makes you even subtly disengage from him and his tears, own it as your personal emotional baggage to work through. While you do, ask him to explain exactly what you can do or stop doing to show your support in his hurting times.

# 55. ▲ ■ ● ◆ ◗ *Be Slave to No Emotions*

*"My younger sister, Stephanie, never ceases to amaze me. Every few months she'll call me and rave on and on about some fantastic man she's started going out with. She always describes them the same way: 'He's so cute . . . ' 'He's very spiritual . . . ' 'He worships me . . . ' and 'He's got it going on . . . ' Then she always sums it all up by saying: 'Girl, I think this is headed somewhere . . . ' Just like clockwork, a few weeks later, Stephanie calls me back, breathing fire. And that same guy is now a selfish, pitiful SOB who's just 'not ready.' To hear Stephanie tell it, every man she ever dated was out to do her harm and she had to 'put them in their place.' Now either all the rotten men in town are lining up outside Stephanie's door waiting on their chance, or my sister is just plain paranoid."*

*—Angela*

Nearly everyone has at least one emotional slavemaster. It's the psychological black hole that you trip into over and over in the normal course of living and loving. It's that troublesome and persistent emotion you feel most intensely, and hate that you feel it, yet you don't quite know *why* you feel it. But you do know it keeps robbing you of happiness. Maybe it's jealousy, or insecurity, or anger, or depression, or resentment, or worry, or . . . Whatever it is, you return there often, even when you try so hard not to. In relationships with men you even try to make them work to keep you from feeling it.

When you are a slave to a particular emotion, you spend huge amounts of time defending yourself, denying the feeling, or demanding your lover order his steps to serve your slavemaster. All of this, of course, leaves precious little time—or energy—for love.

- If you're a slave to insecurity, you won't go forward in love until he takes away all your fears.
- If you're a slave to jealousy, you won't go forward in love until he convinces you that you are better than every woman on the planet.
- If you're a slave to anger, you won't go forward in love until he makes the world, and everyone in it, work just the way you want it to.
- If you're a slave to self-doubt, you won't go forward in love until he becomes your reason for living.

You'll start to measure whether he really loves you by whether or not he succeeds at these awesome and unrealistic responsibilities. When (not if) he fails, you conclude it wasn't real love in the first place, and he's not a true lover anyway. Eventually you will find another love candidate and you and your slavemaster emotion start the process all over again. The truth is that you are stuck in that emotion, and getting unstuck is an inside job.

Your emotional slavemaster has so much power because it's your blind spot. That means you can't see all the hows and whys of it on your own, so you are destined to stay stuck in it.

The emotion that enslaves you won't politely go away on its own. Freedom comes with a fight. I offer you this Emancipation Proclamation: Get some help. Look to someone skilled at helping others get unstuck and freed from emotional slavery. Contact a wise friend, a competent therapist, a minister, or some other qualified coach/collaborator. You deserve it. When you decide to believe that, you will do it.

**Say it:** "I will look on the inside and work on the inside to be free from emotional slavery. I refuse to hold love or lovers responsible to join me in servitude. If I stretch, freedom is within my reach."

**Do it:** Consult with close friends, your medical doctor, and the Yellow Pages to locate the best possible counselor for you. Over the telephone and in person interview them. Take special note of the one(s) with whom you have the best chemistry. When you are ready to get unstuck, follow through on an appointment. Even if it's a sacrifice, do it.

# 56. ▲ ■ ● ◆ ◗
## *Forgive Him, Forgive Yourself*

*"A few days after I came home from the hospital with the baby, I made my hair appointment. I was so depressed about how my hair was looking and all the weight I had to lose—plus, I was dying to get a couple of hours out of the house. Marlon knew how important the appointment was to me and he promised he'd be back from his errands in time to keep the baby. My one o'clock appointment came and went and Marlon hadn't shown, and he didn't even call. I must have gone through every emotion possible within minutes. I was so mad, but at the same time I was worried about him, and by then my cabin fever made me feel like the walls were closing in on me. When he finally got home, nearly an hour late, I was relieved to see him, but I was ready to go off. I barely heard whatever he was mumbling to me about traffic jams, long lines at the bank, and the rest of that blah-de-blah. I thought, 'How could he be so inconsiderate?' It was hard to get over it, because every time I passed a mirror and looked at my hair I got angry at him all over again!"*

*—Billie*

A love that doesn't include forgiveness isn't love at all, it's nonsense. No amount of tender touches, passionate feelings, or heartfelt vows are ever enough when a forgiving spirit is absent. The capacity to forgive him and yourself must be at the core of your relationship.

Forgiveness is seeing failure and misconduct, calling it that, yet refusing to hold the transgressor emotionally hostage till he pays some horrible (and even justifiable) sin tax. Forgiveness is the opposite of punishment. It releases the offender from debt and penalty, and it does so in the name of love.

In great or small ways, you and the man in your life can be counted on, at some point, to screw up. What makes love such a supernatural phenomenon is that, miraculously, two sure-to-fail individuals offer themselves to each other, in the face of failure's inevitability. They can only do that successfully with reliance upon the power of forgiveness.

Men will disappoint you; you will disappoint yourself. Forgiveness does not mean you deny or distort the facts or your feelings, or just go along to get along. That would mean forgiveness is blind, and it most certainly is not.

It's not amnesia that prompts forgiveness, it is the willful choice to pardon the convicted one. Whether it's the Black man you love or the woman holding this book, it is a decision made from pure grace. Grace is the highest form of love.

Finally, forgiveness takes place on two levels: (a) The will level. "I consciously, deliberately release you from owing me your pain in payment for mine." On this level the emphasis is not on what you feel, but what you choose to do. Forgiveness is a choice you make. (b) The emotional level. Feeling forgiving is usually a much slower process than choosing to forgive. Don't rush the feelings, and by all means don't fake it. Be patient. Feelings catch up later. In forgiving, let your will lead and your emotions follow.

**Say it:** "I accept the fact that forgiveness is the nitty-gritty, rubber-meets-the-road part of love. It has little romantic appeal and feels much better received than given. I choose to give it anyway."

**Do it:** Who have you failed, in the past, and desperately sought to be forgiven by? Recall how important it was to you that they forgave you, and exactly how you hoped they would treat you, in spite of how you disappointed or violated them. Try to give your mate a taste of that kind of grace and forgiveness the next time he fails you.

# 57. ■ ◆ ◗ *Learn to Appreciate His "I Love You" Language*

*"Kelvin and I have this little private tradition of making sure to give each other a goodbye kiss and say 'I love you' every time we leave each other. A couple of weeks ago, when it was over a hundred degrees, my air conditioner decides to break down. I didn't even ask him to, but Kelvin came over to see if he could fix it. He spent his whole day in my hot, stuffy house and running back and forth to the hardware store for parts. He worked so hard, and he got that thing working again, just so that I could survive the heat wave. It was pretty late when he left, and Kelvin was just exhausted. Right after he drove off I realized he hadn't kept our goodbye tradition. I called him and said, 'Kelvin, I can't believe you left here without kissing me and saying I love you.' Kelvin didn't miss a beat. He said, 'I told you I loved you all day long—your air conditioner's working isn't it?' Touché."*

*—Deidre*

Men have their own unique "language" to express their love and affection. It's truly a language in that it communicates. It's not strictly a language in the verbal sense, in that it relies less on words, and more on action. Men "speak" volumes of love sonnets by the things they do, rather than the words they recite. If you're not trained to "hear" his language, you'll miss out on all the heartfelt "I love you" messages he's constantly sending you.

Since women have an "I love you" language that relies heavily on nouns, verbs, and adjectives, it can be very hard for you to translate his language, which is almost entirely spoken by what he does, what he's going to do, and what he doesn't ever do. How can two lovers, who each speak a language foreign to the other, ever be sure of each other's love? Both must become bilingual, of course!

Learn to appreciate his "I love you" language and help him to appreciate yours. From time to time drop your native (verbal) language and speak to him in his doing love language. Thank him when he does the same.

You'd never reject a lover who absolutely treasured you, but could only tell you in French, or German, or Swahili. You'd learn enough of his language to recognize when he's speaking words of love, and you'd accept them gladly and be touched by them.

Black men are big on doing. Superior performance, production, output, and upkeep are what matter. Don't be surprised that when it comes to loving you, he operates from the "It's not what you say it's what you do" mind-set. The following are some of the ways he speaks his "I love you" language. There are probably a million others:

- He brings home his paycheck.
- He fixes what's broken.
- He teases and jokes with you.
- He takes on a task that normally is yours.
- He buys you things.
- He protects you.

Recognize that in the doing of these, and countless others, your man is attempting to tell you how deeply he cares for you. When you recognize what he's doing, you'll become overwhelmed by the beauty and the passion of his native language. You'll be able to appreciate that it comes as much from his heart as any words ever could.

**Say it:** "His way of demonstrating 'I love you' isn't any less valuable than my way of saying it. There are so many more loving expressions I receive by watching him, not just listening to him."

**Do it:** At least once a day, for the rest of your life, express your gratitude to the man in your life for the ways he communicates to you when he demonstrates his love for you by the things he does. Be specific.

# 58. ▲ ■ ● ◆ ◗ *Romance Him— Don't Just Wait to Be Romanced*

*"I've had enough. He's got to do better than this. It's the same story almost every Friday night. Nelson shows up to take me out and he hasn't put any thought into the evening. How can a man who is so smart and resourceful on his job not be able to come up with any romantic ideas when we get together? I'm about tired of us sitting in my living room staring at each other. If he really put his mind to it, Nelson could come up with a million ways to sweep me off my feet. But here I sit, still waiting for him to do it."*

*—Josephine*

More often than not, when flowers are sent, chocolates are offered, and romantic evenings planned, it's men doing the sending, offering, and planning. For some mysterious reason when it comes to the tender tasks of romancing a lover, it's mostly men who have to do it, and women who get to receive it. Unfair. It's past time to make that one-way street travel both ways.

One of the major boasts that Black men broadcast amongst themselves has to do with how good they are at wooing and winning the women they love. Romancing you is a job he takes quite seriously. That's why, these days, he is well aware of important romance-related facts like which champagne is the bubbliest, which restaurant is the coziest, and which scenic vista is the most unforgettable.

To men, romance is an art at which they aspire to be masters. Don't be fooled though; as much as he wants to excel at romancing you, he also loves to be romanced.

Face it. When he uses his sensitivity and imagination he dreams up some things, in the name of romance, that have made you feel absolutely adored and practically worshipped. You feel especially loved, because you've been thought about in a special way. Nothing about those wonderful feelings is just because of your gender. Knowing someone loves you enough to dream up delightful ways to show you that love feels good to anybody—him too.

Keep lapping it up from him, let him romance you until your head swims and your toes tingle. Then turn and let him taste the best of your kind of romancing too.

Observe him closely. You'll need to know what pushes his romance buttons. Don't assume they are the same things that push yours. Is he the type who would love for you to share a private beachside sunset with him, or one of your incredible stress-relieving neck massages, with just the right musical accompaniment, or resting his head on your lap while the TV watches him?

Romance is ninety percent knowing what to do and only ten percent actually doing it. Explore and experiment with the ninety percent like a serious-minded research scientist. Do the ten percent like a woman who is crazy in love.

**Say it:** "I have everything it takes to romance him and be romanced by him. I will import and export romance with equal pleasure."

**Do it:** Work regular romantic gestures into your schedule. Start simply, by sending him a fancy note card at his job with nothing on it but your big ruby red kiss and the scent of your perfume.

# 59. ▲ ■ ● ◆ ＞
## *Pay Attention to the Visuals—He Does*

*"Up until then, it was a wonderful evening. I looked like a million dollars, or at least I thought I did, in spite of the fact that I was having a little bit of a Bad Hair Day. Then she walked in. She was not a perfect beauty queen, but it was very obvious to me—and to Michael—that she takes great care of herself. Finally, he*

*says to me, 'Why don't you go over and ask her where she gets her hair done?' I tried to play it off. I couldn't."*

*—Paulette*

Clichés get to be clichés because they've been true for such a long time. For Black men, one cliché that has been elevated to the status of universal law is: "It's not just what you've got, it's what you do with it."

Style, color, grace, sensuality, and beauty mean much to Black men. Remember he's a descendant of African cultures for whom visual presentation is itself a language that communicates on deep levels. Beauty speaks loudly. Black men respond enthusiastically to its voice. You could hear it in the way he said, "You are sooo . . . gorgeous." That time you knew you were—*and* you knew he meant it.

Unlike women, men's initial attraction is greatly based on visual stimulation. He is most motivated to pursue the inner beauty of the woman whose outer aesthetics have already captured his attention. I don't mean you have to be Whitney Houston or Naomi Campbell. I *do* mean you should give yourself the best possible care and let your outside appearance complement all the good inside you.

Commit yourself to giving serious attention to your weight and fitness, hair, skin, and attire. These don't make your beauty—they enhance it. But caution is in order here. Living your life before the mirror, preening and primping nonstop, is not the answer. That makes for bondage, not beauty. Let *balance* be your watchword.

Black men's eyes are their most sensitive sex organs. Make love to his eyes. That's truly safe sex!

**Say it:** "I take responsibility to enhance and maintain the beauty that I hold. I will present my beauty at its best to the Black man I love."

**Do it:** Recall the moment when you were most confident of your attractiveness (a special occasion, wedding, prom night, first date, Sunday morning at church). List the specific external elements that together helped make you feel so assured of your beauty. Decide how to recapture and reincorporate some of those elements into your visual presentation daily.

# 60. ▲ ■ ◆ ◗ *Reject Sexual Myths*

*"I was so green. Thought I knew everything, and didn't know a thing. When I got to college all I knew about sex I had pieced together from eavesdropping on my oldest sister and her friends at sleepovers, and from watching all those Sheba Baby and Cleopatra Jones movies. Pam Grier and all those other sexy actresses would jump in bed with a guy, screw his brains out, then turn around and kill him. It was very easy for me to see that I didn't have what Cleopatra Jones had, and I wouldn't have known what to do with it if I had. That didn't stop me from wishing I did, though."*

*—Rose*

Some of them go all the way back to your elementary school playground. Many were first heard in giggling whispers during big-sister-to-little-sister talks, or from Black superhero movies, or Millie Jackson songs, or women's magazines and the talk shows. They've never done anyone a bit of good, but they have persisted and spread anyway. They are myths, fables, and fairy tales about sex, stupid little lies about one of life's greatest pleasures.

Myths are the convincing untruths that dress up like facts and wander through our lives persuading us to believe them—and setting us up for tremendous disappointments, frustrations, and shame. Sexual myths about Black men, or the women who love them, perpetuate ignorance and cause confusion. For many, sex is already plagued with more than its fair share of half-truths and inaccuracies. To add myths only contributes to even fuzzier understanding.

Size and shape myths, appetite and performance myths, clock myths and calendar myths, what works and what doesn't myths, it's an endless medley of fiction and fable that can cause you to look disapprovingly at your mate—and yourself. Great sex is nearly impossible under these influences.

Anything that unrealistically exalts or debases some aspect of sexuality is dangerous. Myths provide unrealistic measuring sticks and, more often than not, leave one of you or both of you coming up short. Myths are quite effective at making you feel abnormal. On the other hand, the truth about the what and how of sex is very middle of the road. Rest assured you are quite normal.

Don't get too hung up on looking for the threat of sexual myths, lies, and fairy tales. Instead look for the truth. Learning all you can about the nature and quality of truly loving, real-life sex will make you competent to identify the fake stuff.

**Say it:** "I refuse to be in bondage to the sexual myths about Black men or the women who love them. I have become wearied by the damaging effects of them. We shall know the truth, and the truth will make us free."

**Do it:** Sit down with your mate and talk frankly to each other about your standards, expectations, and anxieties as they relate to sex. See if you can identify any of these that may be based on myths that either of you have bought into.

# 61. ▲ *Don't Use Sex as Either a "Sample of" or a "Substitute for"*

*"At first, before Danny and I started having sex with each other, he would call me several times a day, 'just to talk.' We would always go to the beach and lose track of the time, because we'd have these long conversations where we'd talk about everything you could think of. Back then, I hardly minded when we had a problem between us, because we would sit down and discuss it until we worked it out—even if we had to yell and argue some to get it resolved. I know*

*Danny knows how to express himself—we both do—but for some reason, lately it seems like when we have more than five minutes to just sit and check in with each other, before you know it, Danny is turning off the light and undoing my buttons. I barely remember what it's like for us to have a decent conversation anymore!"*

—*Katrina*

Somewhere along the way, the physical side of love has become like some sort of a multipurpose kitchen utensil ("useful for over one thousand purposes"). Some women use it as an introductory offer, allowing a man to try a free sample before he commits to the whole package. Others use sex as a substitute for talking out feelings, or working out problems. ("Let's not fight . . . let's just have sex!") Still others use it merely to cure the doldrums. ("I'm so bored . . . I know, let's have sex!")

The quickest way to wear out a high-quality, simply terrific anything is to use it repeatedly for purposes for which it was not intended. Sex as a "sample of . . ." or a "substitute for . . ." are two such valueless uses. Whenever a good thing gets used for everything, it becomes good for nothing.

Sex is the very special expression of love between the two of you that says "I have a deep and abiding commitment to you, and you to me, therefore I offer you all of me." Sex is because you already have love and commitment. It is not the tool to try to get it. That's why sex is at its best in a committed marriage.

Since men, by nature, highly value masterful performance, for some of them sex can become a kind of proving ground, where they attempt to get reassurance of their worth as a man. Sadly, they have substituted ego-building for lovemaking. Since women, by nature, highly value harmonious and secure relationships, sex can be used to get reassuring "proof" that an intimacy bond exists, when perhaps it doesn't at all.

Your body, and the pleasure of its company, should never be offered carelessly. It's not a free sample, a thirty-day trial, or an investment for future returns. It is never to be used as an acceptable alternative to solid, self-disclosing communication between the two of you.

Sex is not a "you get yours, I'll get mine" thing. It's an "I have received love from you, therefore I want to give myself to you" thing. By making it other than that you make it less than that.

**Say it:** "Making love is not the means to an end, it is an end unto itself. I refuse to use sex as a flashy free sample of who I am, or a convenient substitute for work we need to do to help our love grow."

**Do it:** Have a therapy session with yourself. Place a chair with a photo of yourself (the "client") in front of you (the "therapist"). Confront your client about whatever patterns of sexual "sampling" and substituting have been used by her in past or present relationships. Challenge her to cease. Advise her as to ways she can. Encourage her to be thorough.

## 62. ▲ ■ ● ◆ ◗
## *Don't Put Mama in the Middle*
## *(And Don't Let Her Get There on Her Own)*

*"I mean really . . . she is my mother, and if she needs something and I don't give it to her, where's she going to get it from? Mama always said every wife should keep some money put aside that her husband doesn't know about. When Mama runs a little short, I usually help her out from my stash. But when she wanted me to help her get her new car last month I didn't have enough. I took it from our savings account. The only reason I didn't tell Travis at the time was that I knew he'd go completely crazy on me. Normally he doesn't pay any attention to our bank statements. Of course this month was the one time he did. Now I've got to listen to him accusing me of going behind his back and disrespecting him to please my mother. But Travis knew when I married him that I was very close with my mother."*

*—Lou Ann*

In loving a Black man, Mama—yours or his—can be very much like water. She can be a constant, and deeply refreshing, pool of wisdom and encouragement, beckoning you and the man you love to come and drink whenever you choose. Or she may be like the persistent drip of a leaky faucet, never providing enough to do any good, and leaving a rusty corroded mess in its wake.

Like water, mamas in the wrong place can cause major damage. Mama in the middle of your relationship, controlling, wielding power, and calling the shots is definitely the wrong place. If she's there, help her find her way out.

- If you break promises to him in order to keep promises to her, Mama's in the middle. Usher her out.
- If she can't deal with you unless you are dealing with him her way, Mama's in the middle. Help her to relocate.
- If she knows more of his secrets and sorrows because she heard them from you, not from him, Mama's in the middle. Direct her to the nearest exit.
- If decisions made between you and your man can be altered or abandoned solely because she disapproved, Mama's in the middle. Let her know what time the next train pulls out.
- If one of you, or both of you, look to her to referee your fights, break your ties, or navigate your direction, Mama's in the middle. Escort her out of the area. Immediately.

It's not fair to you, your man, or your mama to allow her in the seat of power in your relationship. It keeps you a child in love and romance, causes him to resent you and the woman who gave you (or him) birth, and makes it too easy for her to be seen as the Wicked Witch of the West to both of you.

Do not be fooled. No matter how much positive, and how little negative, the Black man you love says about your mother, he's always looking for you to be his lover without the excess baggage of a meddling Mama. Too much Mama, in too many places, is too much of an intrusion for many a man to bear.

**Say it:** "Mama is for me to love, respect, and honor. She's my confidante, my advisor, and my anchor. She means far too much to me to let her sit in an unwelcome place in my relationship. I've got a place of honor for her, but it's not in the middle of my man and me."

**Do it:** Stop and think about the things that "just don't feel right" about the role(s) you have given, or allowed, your mother (or his) to take in your relationship. If it doesn't feel right to you, it probably isn't. Commit to taking responsibility for changing what's out of order there. Be brave, be firm, be kind. Above all, don't wait for permission. You won't get it. Don't force change all at once, but by all means get started. Get your power back. Get your priorities in order.

# 63. ▲ ■ ● ◆ )
## *Don't Put Daddy in the Middle*
## *(And Don't Let Him Get There on His Own)*

*"The last place I ever want to be caught again is in the crossfire between my fiancé and my father. They both have ego up the ying-yang. Without even knowing it, I set them off, and they went to all-out war with each other. Perry and I had decided to go to Chicago to spend Christmas with my parents. We had talked about the finances and agreed that driving there would be best. Perry really got into it. He picked up road maps from the Auto Club, and started getting his Bronco in shape for the trip. We were both looking forward to the drive. Three days before we were to leave, Daddy called and told me he didn't want me on the roads for that long a trip. He was sending me—and me only—an airline ticket and told me that he would pick me up at the airport. I knew Perry would be disappointed, but Daddy was just worried about me and I thought Perry would understand. I suggested Perry try to get a seat on the same flight. He was not having it. I could barely explain to Perry before he picked up the phone and called Daddy. It was like a head-on collision. They got it on. They must have both said the words, 'Who do you think you are . . . ?' a hundred times in that conversation."*

*—Rosalind*

If you have the advantage of a close, loving relationship with your father, you have, no question about it, a good thing. The first and best place in life for you to learn the art of how to love a Black man is in your relationship with your father. But, as quiet as it's kept, your relationship with your father is also the place where you can establish some pretty rotten behavior patterns that can work against your love life with a Black man.

Your father's love for you started out being essentially about protection, comfort, and guidance. It can be very difficult for some fathers to let go. They have a hard time seeing you grow up and get those needs met elsewhere. Often a man and his daughter conspire together to keep the "Daddy/Daddy's Little Girl" relationship intact long after it should be. Then when a Black man comes along who wants very much to be the man in your life, it's hard for him to squeeze in, because you've got a security guard named Daddy keeping watch at the gate.

Daddys don't mean any harm, they are only trying to love you, and for them love mostly means protection. Above all Daddy wants to live up to the "Number One Man in Your Life" role. The problem is that the Black man who loves you is dying to fill that same position. Both are motivated by love. Both want to bring their unique brand of strength and caring to your life.

- When the man who gave you life competes with or disregards the man in your love life—Daddy's in the middle and he's got to step aside.
- If Daddy's working overtime, deciding, dictating, and directing your life in general, and your love life in particular, Daddy's in the middle and he's got to vacate that space.
- If the man you love hears so much "Daddy this" and "Daddy that" to make him groan and bristle at the sound of it, Daddy's in the middle and he needs new lodgings.
- If you treat your man as if his opinions and ideas are, in some way, less valid because they don't agree with your father's, Daddy's in the middle and he needs to resign that position effective immediately.

Your Daddy and your man need to meet each other in a place of mutual respect. They have something in common: They both adore you. You have the power, by both your actions and your attitudes, to receive love from them both without alienating either of them.

**Say it:** "I am no longer Daddy's Little Girl. He is no longer the chief hand-holder and dragon-slayer in my life. The man who is my lover cannot steal what belongs to Daddy. I offer him what belongs to me."

**Do it:** In the presence of your father and the man in your life together, describe in detail how they both enrich your life and how much you appreciate their unique roles. Where applicable, respectfully, but firmly, show Daddy out of inappropriate roles or responsibilities (especially those that infringe on your partner's). Reaffirm to them both that you have love enough for both of them equally, but in very different ways.

# 64. ▲● *Don't Play with Marriage (Past, Present, or Future Ones)*

*"Last Saturday my cousin Bridget got married. It must have been the most gorgeous wedding I had ever seen. They really did it up—with the African robes and the drummers. They even jumped the broom at the end. I loved it. Bridget looked so beautiful, and so happy. Being there made me think about my own wedding day, and how I pretty much thought that if we made it through the hassles of the wedding, our love for each other would make the marriage itself a breeze. I thought all those warm romantic feelings would just grow and grow over the years, and we wouldn't have the kinds of struggles that other married couples always tried to warn us about. I sure found out differently. I looked at my cousin and thought: 'Girl, I swear, I hope you know what you are getting yourself into.'"*

*—Joyette*

If you only take a superficial glance at marriage you could easily be fooled into thinking that it's only about lace dresses, ring-swapping, broom-jumping, and cruise-taking. With only a passing glance, marriage can look like such fun and games that you feel you really must play it as soon as you possibly can. Look closer. Underneath it all, marriage is nothing to be toyed with. Not ever.

Since that day when the first caveman and the first cavewoman stood before the first cave preacher to repeat their vows, the sanctity and seriousness of marriage have all too often been ignored. Matrimony has been entered into lightly, and exited from even more lightly. Too often it has been done simply for convenience, a favor between friends, good business, steady sex, a better self-image, or higher status. In these lightweight and inappropriate ways, and a host of others, marriage has been trifled with.

Marriage is a promise to give up the self-satisfying, self-directed, and self-protected life in order to spend your life making someone else's better—even if they can't, or won't always reciprocate. Even if everything about your man and your love for him is perfectly wonderful, if you are not ready to make and keep that kind of promise don't play with marriage.

If you are sure that you are ready, but you aren't certain that the Black man in your life is, slow down and wise up. Take a warning from the old saying, "If it don't fit, don't force it."

CAUTION: In the history of the world some very smart women who love Black men have done some very dumb things when it comes to marriage. Don't be one of those who:

- weren't sure they'd ever be asked, so they married the first man who did—because he did.
- believed some married man who gave them the "My wife doesn't understand me like you do, I'm staying for the sake of the children, but you're really my only true love blah-blah-blah . . ." line.
- expected some poor wreck of a man with a string of failed marriages would marry them and suddenly become Husband of the Year.
- thought that his baby in their womb would guarantee his ring on their finger.
- believed that marriage was the place to hang out while some invisible

Happiness Machine produced happy feelings and happy times. (They also believe when it stopped, so should the marriage.)

**Say it:** "Marriage, for me, is more a promise to give than a means to get. If I see it as anything other than that, I'm settling for something less, but I deserve more."

**Do it:** Consider two or more of the worst marriages (or almost marriages) of which you have close personal knowledge. Try to determine in what ways shallow notions about the nature of marriage could have been a factor in the failure. Consider two or more of the most successfully married couples you know. What do their marriages indicate that they believe about the nature of marital commitment?

# 65. ▲ ■ ● ◆ ☽
## *Love His Children (As Much as You Can)*

*"I guess I expected that Tommy's daughter, Shilene, would love me to death and see me as a second mother. I've always gotten along well with children, and being that Shilene is the child of the man I love, I pretty much assumed that we couldn't help but get along well. I was so wrong. Shilene let me know from the first day we met that she wanted nothing to do with me. She didn't want Tommy to have anything to do with me either. I was heartbroken, especially since Tommy's boys thought I was the best thing going. I tried everything to win Shilene over, but she was not going for it. I had to remind myself that nobody's going to be loved by everybody. After a while, I decided to let her make the first move. If she wants to spend time with me, I'm happy to have her. If not, that'll have to be okay too."*

*—Clarice*

The offspring of the Black man you love must not be strangers to your love. Give them unreservedly your affections, your tenderness, and the strength that comes from mother love, whether you are their mother or not. The man in your life will never know the fullness of your embrace if his children do not too.

It is not necessary to love them in the same ways he does, matching him kiss for kiss, hug for hug, and gift for gift. No, he offers them his brand of devotion, you must offer them yours. The children will savor the sweetness of both flavors.

As far as loving them goes, it matters little if his children are yours or not. Men view their children as parts of themselves. For him, they are actually extensions of his identity. Showering your love upon his kids silently speaks volumes about your commitment to him.

Children are one hundred percent human being. They are never to be used as pawns in working out anything with the man you love. Your relationship with him should never be confused with your relationship with them.

In general, men come a little less adept in the skills of love and affection. No less caring than you, he is still likely to benefit from your example of how to show it. Like no other, you are in the position to demonstrate ways to show that to his children.

**Say it:** "I commit to loving (name the children's names) because of who they are—and because of whose they are."

**Do it:** Tell the man you love exactly what positive traits of his you see in them, and what it means to you. Tell the children.

## 66. ■ ◆ Set Up No Barriers Between Him and His Male Friends

*"Larry plays basketball with some of his frat brothers every Saturday morning— and I do mean* every *Saturday morning. During basketball season they go to all the Bulls home games, and watch the rest of them on TV. These brothers truly stay*

*in touch with each other! That's why I figured it wouldn't be such a big deal for Larry to miss one Saturday to go with me to scout out some yard sales. I had the whole day planned. Just us. I thought it would be fun. I guess, in a way, I wanted to test whether the idea of being with me was attractive enough for him to miss hanging out with the guys, for once in his life. Larry acted like I was asking him to abandon his long-lost twin brother or something. I was too through with him. We went to the yard sales all right—but not until after their game was over!"*

*—Myra*

He may call them his partners, "homies," buddies, or "ace-boon-coons." Whatever. They are his friends, and they are tremendously important to him. He will always need to have some; you will always need to let him.

There is an amazing bond of fellowship that takes place between Black men as they crack jokes (even at each other's expense), laugh, compete, perform a task, solve each other's problems (and those of the whole world), or even when they sit in silence together. Men come away from their times with each other somehow feeling more "man." In the world of friendships, they draw a secret strength that makes them stand sturdier and taller in the rest of their world.

How you respond to his friendships with other men will have great bearing on the quality of the man in your life and the quality of your relationship with him.

Refrain from questioning, judging, or condemning his friends and their friendships. Find ways to nurture his relationships with his friends.

A chief complaint of women who love Black men is that their men overdo friendships with their buddies at the expense of their relationships with the women in their lives. Women cite maximum amounts of his time spent with "the fellas," and minimum amounts with her. It's easy then for women to begin to see men's friendships as a threat to their love relationships. But his friendships are never responsible for keeping the two of you from achieving lasting intimacy. The reasons for that are found within the relationship, not outside it.

Black men need vast amounts of freedom and autonomy. They are at their best emotionally and relationally when they are allowed to regularly go out and experience the free and independent side of their natures. Their prized sense of individuality is nurtured and reinforced in the time they spend with their male friends. They value a sense of intimacy too, and they get it in love relationships with their women. Black men need a steady flow of the former to be fully available to you for the latter. Individuality and intimacy are the two halves that make him whole.

A man's friendships need not be seen as in competition with his love life. When he gets sufficient freedom to be a man among men, he is much more likely to be present and attentive to the woman he loves. To severely criticize his friends, or work to keep him apart from them, will keep the two of you from truly being together.

**Say it:** "His friends are his business. Our relationship and what it takes to make it grow is about us, not them."

**Do it:** Every now and then let yourself be "guilty" of encouraging him to go out (or go away) with his buddies for an afternoon or even a weekend. Surprise them with tickets to a ball game, an auto show, or something like that.

# 67. *Let Him Dream Big Dreams*

*"You would think he would show some appreciation. I mean I tried my best to give him my honest opinion about that crazy idea he had to leave his job and open a video rental store. Can you believe it? If I know a little bit more about those kinds of things than he does, doesn't it make sense that I would try to warn him before he makes a stupid mistake chasing a pipe dream? Then he gets upset with me and starts calling me Miss Discouragement 1996. He doesn't even realize I'm only trying to help. I mean, nobody in their right mind would leave a sure thing like his Post Office job to go after a maybe!"*

*—Lula*

There's no need to ever let your man's dreams frighten you, even if for every noble and ingenious one, he dreams three fantasies of Disney-sized proportions. How he handles his dreams is not nearly as threatening as how he handles reality. He can (and he must) keep a firm grip on reality, and at the same time feel right at home in the world of dreams, ambition, and aspirations. Let him dream big dreams.

Every great thing any man ever did started with a dream. It was something a little bigger than life, yet worthy of his attention and his effort. And many of them are worthy of your enthusiastic endorsement and collaboration. Your contribution to the realization of his dreams can mean the difference between them ending up in the "cheap talk" or "action attempted" file.

Black men possess huge, hardworking, dream-producing machines. They are at work around the clock in a room inside his soul that has I H-O-P-E written on the door. How you handle the dreamer in the man you love has much to do with how much, or how little, greatness he attempts.

Don't always take it upon yourself to play "the voice of reason" with the single-minded determination to snap him out of it and jolt him back into reality. I assure you, lofty dreams and practical reality can peacefully coexist. One is tempered by the other. Do not be intimidated by his dreams.

Let him speak "dream-talk" to you. If he shares his dreams with you, he has welcomed you into the secret chambers of his private world (remove your pumps and tread lightly there). Often he is seeking no more than your ear, and the profound pleasure of having you join him in his exciting exploration of an intriguing possibility.

If asked, give your opinions. If not, don't. Unless the realization of his dreams will directly—and adversely—impact you, take the passenger seat and go along for the ride.

**Say it:** "Who am I to censor, improve upon, or otherwise rearrange his dreams? Although I am never one to ignore harsh reality, neither will I dismiss his lofty dreams. Rather, I will encourage them."

**Do it:** Ask the Black man with whom you have the most significant relationship to explain how the woman who loves him can help him and hurt him when listening and responding to his biggest dreams, ambitions, and aspirations. Encourage him to be specific.

## 68. ▲ ■ ● ◆ ◗
### Don't Let Money or Success Distract You from Love

*"I don't think there's any sister who admits she thinks how much money a man makes or how many things he owns are the only ways to decide if she's interested in him. All of us would like to say those things don't matter very much at all. Every woman I know would swear that if the brother has a good personality and is fairly attractive and considerate, that makes him well worth getting to know and maybe more. Frankly, though, I don't believe any of us would complain if those qualities were found in a man who has some cash too."*

—*Kim*

Be very suspicious of the kind of "love" that is only given to the man who carries a fat wallet, drives shiny cars, wears designer suits, and is known around town. Love that rises and falls based on the stock market is a cheap imitation of the real thing. If you're not careful, money and success (his or yours) can greatly distract you from what matters most.

If his credit report and bank statements elicit more of your passion than his character and style, you are distracted. If you keep saying "Later" to love so that you can chase fame and fortune now, you are distracted. Either way is a good way to miss out on relationships that have some substance, some weight, and some depth.

Money and success are wonderful life-enhancers. They are the glittery results of diligent labor. They are not to be condemned, but neither are they to be used as the standard for assessing a man's potential for love. Besides there aren't enough rich and famous ones available for every woman who wants one.

Women who have to be well-off and well-known before they'll take time to love are deceived. They think that there is a golden day in the future when what she's got and what she's become will be enough to satisfy forever. Then, and only then, she'll look around for romance. That day never comes, or if it does it's a terribly lonely one. Climb the ladder of success, but along the way you should notice that there are some good men at every rung. If you are distracted by the upward trek, you'll miss them and neither of you will know the joys of what could have been.

Grow up. Learn to appreciate some of life's more basic and enduring pleasures: the love and devotion of a good man who may not be able to boast of big bucks, a big name, or large living. Bring your eligibility requirements back down to earth. You can buy your own trinkets and treasures—or get so caught up in everyday blue-collar, working-class love as to not notice their absence.

Don't allow a BMW, an Armani suit, an uptown address, or downtown investments to blind you. Take a chance. Lower your impossibly high standards and "descend" to the level of a hardworking, truly loving Black man who carries riches in his person, but not necessarily in his pockets. One who is ready to generously share with you who he is, not merely what he's got.

**Say it:** "I don't need money and success to make love a pure delight. I will not allow what can vanish overnight to distract me from what can endure for a lifetime."

**Do it:** Talk to your woman friend who is madly in love with an "everyday," as opposed to a "Sunday go to meeting," man. Ask her to share candidly with you about how much or how little her man's financial and social status mean to the quality of their relationship.

# 69. ▲ ■ ● *Fight to Support Your Man— Never to Keep Him*

*"I have never understood what women were talking about when they say things like 'I'm not gonna let that hussy get away with trying to steal my man' or making threats and giving ultimatums to women who might be trying to move in on her husband or boyfriend. It's like they think kicking somebody else's butt is going to keep her and her man together. If it takes all that to keep him, I wouldn't want him anyway. No woman can get anywhere with a man unless that man lets her. I figure, if he wants to stay with me nobody can take him, but going to war with some woman is not going to keep him with me if he wants to go. I am not about to start kicking, scratching, and biting to keep a man around. Not in this life."*

—*Carmen*

Loving a Black man requires that you know exactly when to be "hands on" in demonstrating that love, and when to be "hands off." Although you may sometimes find it difficult to decide on which one when, the two are not mutually exclusive. You do well to do both.

There are some things that are best done standing up and some sitting down. Supporting him is one of the former, trying to keep him is one of the latter. Often, women who love Black men invest far too much time and effort in just trying to keep them, rather than working to build a relationship that is strong and mutually affirming.

The motivation to claw, scratch, or maim any other woman to ensure that your man stays your man comes from a fearful, insecure part of your being. The inspiration to support and champion his cause comes from millennia of accumulated strength and power, there inside your soul. You are always at your best when you walk in power, rather than fear. Let your power be used to fortify him and to undergird him, not just to constrain him to stick around.

Do everything you can to make him a constant witness of your willingness to let him draw from the pools of your strength.

You are worth more than having a man who sticks around only because he "should," "ought to," and "must." You deserve one who's there with you because that's exactly where he wants to be. Your loving and supportive ways can be powerful motivators for him to remain committed to love and to gladly linger with you. Too often, listless lovers use the threat of their imminent departures to exploit, frighten, or control their women. Give him a surprise. Let him know, "I'd love you to stay, but if you've got to go, go!"

**Say it:** "It is not mine to fight anyone or anything to keep the man I love. Keeping power is inside his love for me, not inside my anger or my fear."

**Do it:** If you were your own therapist, what insight would you give yourself on the subject of the fear of being alone? Why? Honestly examine how your insights relate to you, and how you operate with the men in your life.

# 70. ▲ ◆ *Take Your Time—Slow Down, Don't Rush*

*"When I was seventeen, I had no problem waiting and letting nature take its course. I had to wait for my skin to clear up, wait for my parents to let me go out with boys. I waited, and waited some more, for one of them to ask me—then I waited to find out if he was going to act right or not. Now I wait for the phone to ring. I spend more time than I want to, waiting. All that may be fine at seventeen, but at my age, sitting back and waiting on something to happen means I end up*

*spending too many Friday nights with Jay Leno and a pint of Häagen-Dazs ice cream."*

—*Addie*

There is an unfortunate tendency on the part of the whole human race to rush the things that we delight in most. If it's good, we want it right now or, better still, yesterday. Some of life's very best stuff is stuff we want to have, handle, and hold quick, fast, and in a hurry. We go to Christmas parties in November, we munch popcorn that takes only seconds to pop, we rush to wear today what we can't pay for until next year. Love is a good thing, and if you're not careful, it too will become a rushed thing. Take your time.

At every stage of a love relationship with a Black man, you'll need to work hard to avoid "microwave madness," the frantic rush to meet "him" today and get to the "happily ever after" part by tomorrow. Slow down. Give him, yourself, and your relationship the chance to develop deeper roots, and a sturdier foundation than can be produced overnight.

This is no call to procrastinate, meander, or retreat. Unnecessary delay is not your friend. Don't stop any positive forward movement, but don't rush so much that you miss all the sweet, progressive steps along the way, speeding to the finish line.

You are rushing way too fast if you spend more time worrying about how long the kind of love you want is taking than enjoying the kind of love you already have.

Don't be alarmed if Mr. Right didn't jet into your life today. Maybe he's on his way by boat, or bus, or bike. Be patient.

Don't lose your calm if head-over-heels love didn't bloom this season, or if rebuilding a fallen love takes more than a day, a week, or a month.

Decide you will slow down and wait. Don't get obsessed with arrival at the destination, savor the thrill of the ride.

**Say it:** "A deep, rich, satisfying love that can be counted on to endure is what I want. It's not available in instant, ready-mixed, or quick-drying forms. I can, I will, I must, slow down."

**Do it:** Identify the area of your love life about which you have the most anxiety and the biggest tendency to rush. List on paper the fear(s) you have that tempt you to rush. For a week or longer, set a specific time of the day to worry about that. Worry then and there only. Outside of that time, force yourself to slow down and be calm about it.

# 71. ▲ ■ ● ◆ ◗
## *Use Your Strengths, Work on Your Weak Areas, Admit Your Failures*

*"I always tell myself, I'm going to learn from my mistakes, and get on with my life. Of course, that's easier said than done. I have a habit of beating myself up pretty hard when my relationships go bad—especially when I know I could have handled myself, or the situation, better than I did. I'm sure nobody makes all the right moves, says all the right words, or chooses the right guy all the time; but I still feel pretty terrible when I've jumped out there and forgotten to use my head. I haven't given up on myself yet though. One of these days I am going to realize that I may not be as good at this love thing as I'm going to be, but I am so much better at it than I used to be. And I'm not finished yet!"*

*—Trinette*

What's the one thing in this life that you know, beyond a shadow of doubt, that you do well? Don't be shy. What have you become unquestionably great at? Writing touching letters? Winning marathons? Raising perfect kids? Running a corporation? Hosting incredible parties? Whatever it is, if you chart the path of your success in it, you will notice that in that area of your life you are intimately aware of your strengths, your weaknesses, and your failures—and your unique ability to work with them, around them, and in spite of them to achieve your goals. To succeed at love with a Black man you'll need to bring those same characteristics to the task.

Love has no recipe that works in every circumstance, always guaranteeing a light, fluffy, sweet-tasting relationship. Just like with the "Number One Incredible Thing You Do," successful relationships involve much more trial and error than we often care to acknowledge. It's effort and activity over time that make for a mutually satisfying relationship.

Anything that takes effort and activity over a period of time means you will be good in some areas (your strengths), only adequate in some others (your weak areas), and in yet others, a "sho-nuff" screw-up (your failures).

Focus on your strengths, know them well enough to be able to exploit them for all they're worth. The many, the few, or even the one thing that you do well in the world of love make up your strong suit. You should play them like trump cards in a hot bid–whist game. Your strengths balance out many of the flaws in your style and can provide you a winning hand in spite of those flaws.

Give yourself the space and the time to work on your weaknesses. Wherever they are—in your personality, your emotions, your style of relating, or the technical skills of loving. With effort, some of them will gradually become strengths, some will improve just a bit, and some won't budge at all. Don't let that throw you. Remember the "Number One Incredible Thing You Do"? Your weak areas challenged you, but they haven't kept you from succeeding.

Refusing to admit your failures, or to never study them in order to draw out the valuable lessons they hold, is like owning a diamond mine and locking yourself out of it. To fail proves that you are human. Welcome to our little club. To look boldly at your failures and learn from them means you are a pretty exceptional human being—and that you plan to try again.

**Say it:** "Just as I see the world in three dimensions, I will look at my style of loving and relating to men that way as well. I will proudly wear my strengths, work to shore up what's weak, and follow my failures toward self-improvement and away from self-condemnation."

**Do it:** Divide a long sheet of paper into three columns headed "My Strengths," "My Weak Areas," and "My Failures." Reviewing your past and present relationships with men, chart the characteristics about you that apply under each heading. Take at least thirty minutes to boast out about what's in the first column, strategize steps to improve in the second, and identify the most beneficial lessons from the third.

# 72. Learn to Live with Mystery

*"It took me the longest time to get with the idea of moving. I loved our house, and I had worked so hard to make it look like what I'd always imagined it could. Then leaving our neighbors, the kids' friends, their schools . . . I had a fit about it at first. But my husband, Jason, kept saying now is the time to make the move to the suburbs. He said I was being sentimental and overly emotional. He was preaching about low interest rates, larger square footage, and resale values. I had never seen him so hyped up before. So we looked around and quickly found what Jason called 'The Castle.' He immediately started trying to convince me this was our dream home. The place was to die for. That and Jason's sales pitch finally won me over. I got caught up in his enthusiasm, and started bringing home boxes. The day before we were to open escrow on 'The Castle' Jason came home and announced, ever so calmly: 'We'd be crazy to leave this house and our good neighbors so we can move out to some boring suburb. I think we should stay right where we are.' You could have knocked me over with a feather. How he got from 'gotta go' to 'gotta stay' that fast, I will never know."*

*—Delcie*

Even if you've pored over every word of this book, and followed its advice to the letter, you will find Black men (and especially your own) will still have some mysterious and unknown "X factors" that you just won't understand about them. You'll not be rid of every question you ever had about how to love them either. In some ways they will always be a mystery to you. Let me share a secret: You can live (and love) just fine with mystery.

None of us can stand not being able to explain the things that baffle us. That's why we read the last page of a murder mystery before we read the first, and fast-forward suspenseful movies to the climax. We are certain that we will evaporate, or melt, or simply die, if we don't quickly get neat tidy answers to the unknowns of life. The truth is, there are some things about men for which no neat tidy answers exist. They are, and to a degree, will always remain, a mystery to women.

One of the biggest attractions between men and women is the fact that they can never fully sum each other up. No matter what discoveries you make, on some questions you will still be left groping in the dark for answers. Getting bored with each other is much less likely to happen when a little mystery remains between you. Learn to live with it.

Don't get nervous. Don't run and hide. Don't bang your head against a wall. When you can't understand him *and* love him, then just love him.

If you try too hard to figure him out, you'll break out in hives and be tempted to turn your lover into a research project, or a game of 20 Questions. Both of which are a pointless bore for you, and a real turnoff for him.

Relax. Some answers to his perplexing ways will come later, and some not at all. If you accept that, his mysteries will gradually become less alarming and much more appealing—and maybe even enticing. He will prove to be just understandable enough to catch your attention, and complex enough to keep it.

**Say it:** "At the same time that I learn how to love a Black man, I practice how to live comfortably with what I'll never understand about him."

**Do it:** Practice loving your Black man in the here and now. Whenever you become anxious, impatient, or otherwise at a loss to make sense of him, say aloud: "It's a mystery, and at this moment, that's okay."

# 73. ▲ ■ ● ◆ ☽
## *Expect to Get Tired, Expect to Get Strong*

*"I'm at the gym four or five times a week. I enjoy aerobics and weightlifting especially. I have gotten in pretty good shape, if I do say so myself. Judy, my trainer, says getting fit and building strength is all about lifting your maximum amount of weight over and over to the point of failure—to the point at which you are so exhausted you feel like you can't lift even one more time. Then, she says, the trick is to try to lift one more time anyway. Judy says that's the only way muscles get solid and strong."*

*—Lula*

The hard part about coming to the end of an advice book like this one is that your leisure reading will soon be over, and you'll be squarely faced with the challenge to do something. Whatever something(s) you need to do to love a Black man better (for him and for you) means change. Change upsets the hell out of us. Change means effort, hard effort. Hard effort exhausts us. Even now, knowing that you're only a page or two from the end of this book, you may feel a growing anxious discomfort moving around your insides. Your well-read brain has sent an all-points bulletin throughout your system saying: "BOOK ENDING. PREPARE FOR EXERTION. PREPARE FOR CHANGE!"

Learning is never enough. Merely learning is filling up the tank with fuel and never getting on the freeway. Living what you've learned is another matter altogether. I really want you to live what you've learned here. Because I really want you and some Black man, somewhere, to have a love that's glorious and makes the rest of the world know that it's really possible.

For that to happen you'll have to embrace the process of change. Expect your effort at it to make you tired and, paradoxically, to make you strong. You will, simply because you work for it, become fully equipped and able to develop and maintain the kind of love you deserve.

Don't procrastinate. Don't "if, and, or but" yourself out of it. Don't talk a good game, and then never get around to playing one. Expect to get tired of trying to love a Black man. Fatigue is always temporary. Expect to get stronger and become more fit for the job. Strength endures.

Do it for yourself. Do it for him. Do it for a change, but by all means, do it *now*.

**Say it:** "I am committed to making lessons learned, lessons lived. What makes me weary, won't make me weak."

**Do it:** Go back through this book reflecting on the Satisfaction Actions that have the most personal relevance for you. After making a list of those, number them in order of priority for you to work on. Commit to no more than three at a time to diligently work on until you become strong in them, then move to another set. Set your pace, keep your focus, and above all, let yourself be very proud of your demonstrated commitment to the Black man you love and to yourself.

## For More Information

*How to Love a Black Man* was inspired by the many men and women throughout the country who have experienced powerful transformations in their relationships after attending Dr. Ronn Elmore's highly successful seminars.

Dr. Elmore is available for lectures, conferences, seminars, and other speaking engagements, inspiring his audiences on a variety of topics related to love, marriage, and personal motivation, especially as they relate to African-Americans.

To contact Dr. Elmore please call or write:

Dr. Ronn Elmore
Relationship Enrichment Programs
1439 W. 94th Street
Los Angeles, CA 90047
(213) 779–8447